KEN LIVINGSTONE was born into a family of working class tories in 1945. He left school without political convictions and only joined the Labour Party at the age of 23. In the seventies he worked as a local councillor in both Lambeth and Camden, becoming a full-time GLC councillor in 1974 and leader in May 1981. Seen both as a future Labour Party leader and as the natural successor to Tony Benn on the Labour left, Livingstone's urbane style and sober political analysis has earned him political respect and support on the one hand, and the animosity of a large section of Fleet Street and the Conservative Party on the other. His hobbies include the cinema, natural history, science fiction and walking.

TARIQ ALI was born in Lahore in 1943. He was educated in Pakistan and came to Oxford in 1963 where he studied Politics, Philosophy and Economics, at Exeter College. He was editor of the *Black Dwarf* and the *Red Mole* during the late sixties and early seventies. He has written on current affairs for the *New Statesman*, *New Left Review* and *The Guardian* (London), and is the author of a number of books, the most recent of which include *1968 and After* (1978), *Trotsky for Beginners* (1980) and *Can Pakistan Survive?* (1983). He is a member of the editorial board of *New Left Review*.

Ken Livingstone

In Conversation with

Tariq Ali

Verso

Who's Afraid of Margaret Thatcher?

In Praise of Socialism

British Library
Cataloguing in Publication Data

Tariq Ali
    Who's Afraid of Margaret Thatcher?
    1. Livingstone, Ken 2. Politicians—
    England—London—Biography
    I. Title II. Livingstone, Ken
    942.1085′092′4   DA676.8.L5

The two interviews contained in this volume were conducted at County
Hall, London in June 1983 and April 1984. The first of these originally
appeared in *New Left Review* 140, July–August 1983.

First published 1984
© Ken Livingstone, Tariq Ali and Verso Editions 1984

Verso Editions
15 Greek Street London W1V 5LF

Filmset in Plantin by
PRG Graphics
Redhill, Surrey

Printed in Great Britain by
The Thetford Press Ltd,
Thetford, Norfolk

ISBN 0 86091 094 6
        0 86091 802 5 pbk

For Tony and Caroline Benn

Contents

Labourism and the Pink Professors
By way of an introduction
Tariq Ali

These are hard times. Capitalism's classic response to its own crisis, mass unemployment, has divided and demoralized the workers movement. The fear of further job-losses has paralysed a significant majority of trade-unionists.

The 1984 miners' strike is, at the time of writing, not yet over, though, given the isolationist mood of the workers, it seems destined at best, to produce a stalemate. If it were to be savagely defeated, then the existing passivity would receive a further impetus. None of this is particularly surprising. Unemployment, on this large scale, does not create a corresponding radicalization| of working-class consciousness. There are always minorities which can and do begin to pierce the cocoons of bourgeois mystification, much stronger in Britain than in continental Europe. What is normally required, however, is a lead from the political parties of the Left. During the Thirties, the Communist Party and the Independent Labour Party played a major part in campaigning against unemployment, war and fascism. This was a period which, in most respects, was much worse than the present. Yet resistance was considered vital in order to renew the workers movement and prepare it for resuming the offensive. The defeat inflicted on the supreme war leader Churchill by the Labour Party in 1945 was, partially, a result of the struggles that had polarized Britain in the Thirties.

The present crisis has been made much worse by the intervention of our pink Professors and their even paler house-journals. Their pathetic prescriptions are a combination of defeatism and masochism. They preach endless sermons on the iniquities of the new Labour left and its best known spokespersons, Tony Benn and Ken Livingstone. They advise nothing but caution, 'realism' and permanent retreat. Their solutions are banal in the extreme, laced with a jargon designed to please the manufacturers of public opinion. They have learnt little from the debilitating experience of the Wilson and Callaghan years.

Bernard Crick, Professor of Politics at Birkbeck College in London, tells us that Labour's tragedy lies in the fact that the new influx of members in the Constituency Labour Parties (CLPs), instead of being treated to 'sobering buckets of cold water' (which, Birkbeck students tell one, are a speciality of the Professor) were, instead, subjected to the horrors of Bennism:

> Benn spoke to these new folk, not to get them to grapple through socialist theory with the hard problems of egalitarian aspirations . . . but to flatter them in a Chartist or populist manner that every hard issue and dilemma of policy could be turned into a question of democratic control by the people . . .

Much worse follows, though in similar vein. At the end of all this flatulence all we are left with are a few toadying references to Neil Kinnock, together with the following:

> Rhetoric, said great Aristotle, must enunciate simple principles, be based on empathy with the actual audience addressed, and must find forms appropriate to persuading that audience. If the Labour Party is to save itself, it must practise rhetoric in that sense, not premeditated propaganda: it must come out of its internal debates and talk to ordinary people everywhere – at every level, on every occasion and through every medium . . .
>
> Neil Kinnock is a socialist with a broad perspective. If anyone can talk to both Party and country, restore argument from principles rather than programme and stimulate serious debate about the timescales and

stages appropriate for different goals, convey both purpose and realism, it is he . . . [1]

The Professor does not elaborate as to whether Kinnock's socialism is as broad as that of his (Crick's) dead hero, Ernest Bevin, who played such a vital role after learning the art of politics as Churchill's office-boy and later became the main British architect of NATO. Pragmatism has always been the common-sense of the Fabian intelligentsia, but surely this latest display of political weightlessness must be embarrassing even for the fellow-denizens of Crick's political world.[2]

A far more coherent and more right-wing strategy for Labour has, in fact, been mapped out by a former senior-common-room colleague of Bernard Crick. In a series of sustained polemical interventions, published in *Marxism Today* and excerpted in *The Guardian*, Eric Hobsbawm, a leading Communist Party historian, has assailed the perspectives of the Labour Left and put forward his version of 'socialist realism'. His repeated forays have won him countless plaudits from leader-writers and political pundits in *The Guardian*, *Observer* and *Financial Times*, as well as grateful applause from the Labour Right. Hobsbawm's opinions have been given prominence not because of any intrinsic merits they might possess, but because he has emerged as the most articulate defender of the consensual establishment that dominated Britain's political culture and its cultural politics from 1940 to 1979. This establishment, which comprises the Liberal Party, the BBC, the SDP, sections of Fleet Street as well as the Labour Right and Centre, was thrown into total

---

1. Bernard Crick, 'The Future of the Labour Party', *The Political Quarterly*, Vol. 54, No. 4, October – December 1983.
2. A word of advice for the good Professor. He should abandon trying to look for new Bevins, (cf 'Ernest Bevin, Foreign Secretary' *New Statesman*, 30 December 1983). Times have changed. Even the Right would today be embarrassed by Bevin's crude cold-war utterances and his slavish adulation of Churchill. He should, instead, link up with the new careerist politicians of the Labour Co-ordinating Committee (LCC) and help search for more subtle methods of achieving his objectives.

confusion by Thatcher's firm repudiation of the old consensus. They began to lose supporters to the new Conservatism (Paul Johnson, Hugh Thomas), and they remain
fearful that unless the tide is reversed, an explosive response
from the socialist Left will become difficult to contain. The
changes that have already begun to transform the Labour
Party are only the first dramatic confirmation of their ner-
vousness.

At a time when none of the ideologues of the old establishment was offering much more than factional propaganda for
their respective gang (Shirley Williams, David Owen, Peter
Jenkins; Michael Foot, Ian Aitken; Denis Healey, Peter
Kellner; Roy Hattersley, Alan Watkins, Anthony Howard,
etc), the advent of Eric Hobsbawm must have appeared as a
sign from above. It was, of course, a situation replete with
irony. A distinguished Marxist historian and an oldtime
Communist coming to the rescue of a beleaguered, exhausted
and discredited cavalry? We will resist all temptations to
dwell further on these ironies or to trace their lineage. Far
more important to discuss the political content of
Hobsbawm's analysis.

It would be both foolish and counter-productive to dismiss
all of Hobsbawm's recent work simply because one disagrees
with his political conclusions. He has pointed correctly to
some of the peculiarities and weaknesses of the British
Labour Movement. He has stressed the continuing decline of
working-class support for Labour. He has insisted that conditions of severe economic crisis do not automatically result
in a shift to the left. Only a fantasist would disagree. Where
Hobsbawm is wrong, and dangerously so, is in his view that
the only solution to the present crisis lies in a historic com-
promise between Labour and all other anti-Thatcherite
forces in British politics. A Grand Coalition to resolve the
current impasse. He does not go so far as to say that
Thatcher's rule *is* fascism, but the desperation underlying his

strategy recalls the old CP line of the Popular Front, a tactic, alas, which ended in tragic failure in Spain and France. Nonetheless, if it is continually argued that the only alternative to Conservatism (vintage 1979–84) is a return to the consensus of 1940–79, then logic and good sense dictate a particular choice of alliances. An alliance against Thatcher would, of necessity, start with Edward Heath, Francis Pym, Ian Gilmour and extend via Davids Steel and Owen to Kinnock/Hattersley. Prior to the Falklands war, serious sections of ruling-class opinion were toying with precisely such a proposition. It was a period when the media's romance with Hobsbawm had reached a blissful peak, and there are clear signs at the moment that it has started to blossom again.[3] There is, however, one major problem. The majority of the Right and the Left in the Labour Party are, at the moment, not prepared to consider any bloc with the Alliance or the Heathites. There are, of course, precedents as far as parliamentary arrangements are concerned. Callaghan organized a Lib–Lab pact, and nice old Michael Foot (as Callaghan's deputy) set up a deal with those shining examples of humanity and rationalism, the Ulster Unionists. No doubt a minority Labour Administration would be prepared to consider similar measures *if* they win the largest number of seats in 1987–88, though a lot will depend on the composition of the new Parliamentary Labour Party. It is unlikely that a parliamentary alliance which excluded the removal of Cruise and Trident, or sought to cover up fundamental differences on private education and the National Health Service, would muster a decisive majority in the PLP.

Even if we accept, for the sake of argument, that the 'rainbow circle' advocated by Hobsbawm/*Marxism Today*, Labour MP Frank Field and Lord Young of Dartington does

3. This is, of course, ignoring such minor hiccups as the role of an independent Communist Party and how poor Gordon McLennan would figure in such a configuration.

become a reality, the basic question remains unsolved. What will such an alliance implement in the field of practical policies. It might well promise pots of gold buried at the extremities of the rainbow but, Crick apart, who will believe these promises? Hard times, I know, have a terrible effect on individual and collective memories. Socialists are not in business to encourage political amnesia. The years of Labourism were not a golden age. It is impossible to understand the lurch to the Right in contemporary Britain without any reference to the preceding Labour Governments of Wilson and Callaghan. The Keynesian compact was buried hurriedly by Margaret Thatcher, but the grave-diggers had been at work for some time before 1979. Monetarist budgets to create unemployment, severe cuts in social expenditure, confrontation with the unions, belly-crawling before Nixon-Kissinger: all this was the stock-in-trade of traditional Labourism. Hardly surprising, then, that the Labour front-bench was virtually immobilized during Thatcher's first term. Every time they mildly criticized some Tory proposal, a jubilant and cynical Tory would exclaim that the government was merely acting on plans inherited from Labour.

The 1966 Labour Government had won an impressive majority. It had received the second-largest popular vote in its entire history, and its 363 seats, were only thirty short of the total it won in 1945. It had a 'safe' majority, but safe to do what? The Labour Left had argued in 1964–66 that radical reforms, nay, socialism itself, were hampered by the minuscule majority of three in 1964. They had pleaded with party activists and their own consciences that the 'boat should not be rocked' until Labour had a larger majority. Foot and *Tribune* continued to regard Wilson as a Prime Minister of the Labour Left.[4] In the event, Labour's massive majority was

4. At a Labour Club meeting in Oxford in 1965 some of us challenged Foot to explain why Tribune MPs could not pressure Wilson on Vietnam, as the right-

used to reinforce Wilson's previous policies, described accurately by the *Financial Times* as 'bombing the communists in Vietnam, bashing the trades unions and keeping blacks out of Britain'. There was no organized opposition to Wilsonism from within the PLP. The leaders of the *Tribune* group were simply incorporated into the Government, Foot merely being the last in line, a punishment for his conference attacks on Labour's foreign policy in the 1964–70 period. It was the frontal assault on trade-union rights and a blatantly pro-capitalist incomes policy that led to a widespread disillusionment with Labour within the working class. Wilson admitted as much on television the day after the defeat of 1970. It is that defeat from which Labour has yet to recover. Its electoral victory in the two general elections of 1974 was the result of a biased electoral system. The popular vote had already reached a low ebb under Wilson. Nothing that he or Callaghan did in the 1974–79 phase was designed to win back the lost millions.

The Heath government attempted to base itself on the Selsdon Programme, which was a hardline set of policies designed to curb union power as a prelude to capitalist rationalization plans. But Heath could not carry through a new course for British capital: his plans foundered on the rock of working-class militancy, symbolized by the miners' strikes of 1972 and 1974. Heath retreated in the face of this pressure and lost the 1974 election, by a narrow majority. Wilson, Callaghan, Healey and Foot failed to capitalize on Labour's policies by implementing the radical set of measures agreed by party and unions. Instead they paved the way for Thatcher to succeed where Heath had failed. This Labour failure was to have a profound impact on working-

---

wingers Desmond Donnelly and Woodrow Wyatt had done to prevent the re-nationalization of the steel industry. Foot exploded: 'Don't you people realize that Wilson is the most left-wing Prime Minister we'll ever get.' This was not intended as a reflection on the limitations of capitalist democracy.

class perceptions. It had antagonized skilled and craft sectors of the workers by attempting to redistribute wealth within the working class, but it had still failed to satisfy the City of London. British capitalism required a ruthless plan of action to increase profits, regardless of the social consequences. In the new model Conservative Party it found a perfect instrument, and in Thatcher a hard-nosed leader unaffected by patrician hang-ups. As a consequence, some of the more vital sectors of British capitalism are doing extremely well out of the crisis.[5] The coffers of the Tory Party remain full, a sure sign that it has not isolated itself from mainstream capitalism. In other words, the material basis of Keynesian reformism has been eroded by the present crisis, something which David Owen understands perfectly well.

Those who argue that what is holding back a Labour recovery is the lack of a deal with the Alliance have to explain why the same coalition lost in 1979. It was that defeat that laid the basis for a sea-change in British politics. The fundamental recomposition of British politics which was inaugurated by Thatcher continues to take place. Its pace is sometimes painfully slow, but the currents which emerged in 1979–80 have not disappeared. The Alliance continues to get a sizeable vote in the South-East: the election of Labour's 'dream-ticket' has not brought the voters flocking back to the Labour Party. The media explanation for this is that Kinnock is not sufficiently right-wing and only a firmness towards the unions and a political bloc with the Alliance could deliver the goods.[6] The political basis of any such accord is never specified, but it is hardly a secret. What is

5. An extremely effective rebuttal of the Hobsbawm/*Marxism Today* theses on the 'irrationality' of Thatcherite policies is contained in John Ross, *Thatcher and Friends*, London, 1983.

6. This variant of the Hobsbawm argument was put forward within the space of a few days by Alan Watkins in *The Observer* (13.5.84), Hugo Young in *The Guardian* (14.5.84), Frank Field, MP, on the Agenda Page of the latter newspaper on the same day, and Adam Raphael in *The Observer* (20.5.84). This never-ending refrain shows no sign of disappearing.

being proposed is a new trendy version of Labourism without the unions. The SDP was, after all, formed not simply to offer a 'moderate' alternative to Conservatism, but to popularize American-style politics in this country. During the 1983 election campaign Thatcher herself promoted this theme at one stage, but changed her stance later in the campaign and suggested that the Labour Party was a permanent feature on the landscape and could not be written off. The most noticeable feature of the SDP's domestic policies is its hostility to the trade unions: it was critical of the Tebbit 'reform' proposals from the right, arguing that his restrictions on collective bargaining were insufficient to deal with the problem. It is this that separates the SDP from the Healey/Hattersley wing of the Labour Party, and it is not just a cosmetic rift.

Yet Hobsbawm is correct when he suggests that there are important points of unity, which could form the basis for common action. Heath and Pym, Owen and Steel, Healey and Hattersley have all defended soft monetarism, wage restraint, the antediluvian structure of British political institutions, NATO as the pivot of the Western Alliance, and the retention of nuclear weapons. If these people were to get together, they would exclude Thatcher, Tebbit, Howe, Brittan, et al. from the Government. But would they themselves represent a meaningful alternative to the present regime? We should not forget that the economic crisis has now made 25 million workers unemployed in the advanced capitalist states alone. Neither the French nor the Spanish government has been able to reverse the trend, and one of the dire consequences is that fascism has once more become an important current in France. It is doubtful that Hobsbawm's projected coalition could stem the tide in Britain. Experience, after all, suggests other lessons, which the Labour Left has learnt the hard way. This brings us back to something which too many of the Shadows who sit on the Opposition Front Bench are trying to forget: the Labour *Party*.

Prior to the Falklands War, it was generally stated that Thatcher's electoral defeat would result in a hung parliament, thus accelerating tensions within the Labour Party between traditional Labourists and the new Socialists. The re-making of the party had proceeded at a fairly rapid pace since the 1979 defeat. Trade union anger and CLP bitterness at what had been done combined to produce a major change in the Party constitution. The almost total autonomy and unaccountability of the PLP was seriously weakened, and frightened MPs elected Michael Foot rather than Denis Healey to replace Callaghan. Labour's parliamentary caucus had acted in the knowledge that it was no longer supreme. A leading SDP apologist was subsequently to suggest that it was Foot's election which precipitated the defection of four former Labour Cabinet ministers, all of whom had happily served with Foot in Callaghan's administration. In a frank and friendly exchange with Sam Aaronovitch and Stuart Hall in the Eurocommunist magazine, *Marxism Today*, Peter Jenkins, a *Guardian* leader-writer and columnist, stated:

PJ But Sam, let me say something, speaking as an out-and-out reformist, in the presence of you socialists and Marxists. Stuart asks what snapped. Well I think what snapped was that a number of people came to the conclusion that the *broad church of the labour movement* (my italics–TA) was no longer a viable vehicle for what came to be called 'social democracy'. This element in the Labour Party, all through the Sixties and still, although by now against the odds, in the Seventies, saw the best prospect for the Labour Party as an out-and-out and explicitly reformist, you might say non-socialist, party along the lines of the German SPD. That was what they wanted to see . . .

The people who led the breakaway had come to believe in 1980 that it would not be possible to retrieve the situation unless, say, two out of three conditions were met. One was that the democratization surge was resisted and the leadership remained the prerogative of the Parliamentary party or was decided on a one-person, one-vote basis. Secondly certain policies that were unacceptable to these people had to be reversed: notably withdrawal from the Common Market, unilateral nuclear disarmament and the alternative economic strategy. Thirdly there was the leadership itself. Once Foot became leader, I think this was the clincher and they realized that under his leadership the battle was lost and they got out.[7]

Since 1945, the anti-Tory coalition had been constituted inside the Labour Party. It was this that made Labour Governments a crucial pillar of capitalist democracy in Britain, an important mainstay of a constitution that is part-oligarchic and part-mystical. Traditional Labourism came to represent a governing order of three interrelated elements. The myth of unity embodied in the utterly counterfeit concept of the 'broad church'; a first-past-the-post electoral system that underpinned the privileges of the 'broad church'; and a completely corporate relationship to the working class, symbolized by the system of block-votes on the level of organization, which helped to preserve the stability of the *status quo* against the CLPs. This anti-Tory coalition was shattered by the experience of the post-1964 Labour Governments, which were incapable of confronting, leave alone defeating, the real wielders of power in Britain. Incapacities such as these are rarely tested in periods of economic boom and full employment. It is largely during recessions that they acquire an explosive potential. Wilson and Callaghan repeatedly told themselves that Labour was now a 'party of government' and consistently promised the City of London that only Labour in office could contain the working class via vertical integration between government and trade-union leaderships.[8] The failure of Wilson's *In Place of Strife* anti-union proposals and Callaghan's inept handling of the 1978 'winter of discontent' made both leaders dispensable as far as ruling-class interests were concerned.

All these episodes, however, left their mark inside the Labour Movement. The Jenkins/Williams section of the

7. Peter Jenkins, Stuart Hall and Sam Aaronovitch, 'Redrawing the Political Map', *Marxism Today*, December 1982.
8. Cited in David Coates, *Labour in Power*, London 1980.

Labour Right felt stifled by their party's umbilical links with organized labour. They wanted a stand-up fight with the unions regardless of the consequences. They felt that this was the only way in which the City of London and the international banking system could be convinced of Labour's ability to manage late-capitalism. The SDP had already been born when Callaghan was elected leader of the Labour Party. For Roy Jenkins's faction it was Callaghan who represented the worst aspects of the union-party link: the subsequent election of Foot and the Wembley conference decisions were merely a useful ideological cover for their total withdrawal from any form of working-class politics. The trade-unions were disenchanted with the old regime for their own reasons. Wilson's disgraceful witch-hunt against the National Union of Seamen in 1966[9], Callaghan's vendetta against the Fire Brigades Union in 1977, and the attempt by both Prime Ministers to restrict wages rather than dividends, were perceived as blatant acts of betrayal. It was the withdrawal of working-class support that lost Labour the 1970 elections; it was the decision of a few million trade-unionists to vote for Thatcher that led to Callaghan's defeat in 1979. In order to defend the record of these governements, Denis Healey has repeatedly stressed that the defeat of Labour did not result in a massive swing to the left and that neither the CP nor the far-left groups made any real gains as a result. This is true. Only a fool could have imagined that any of the left groups represented an electoral alternative to the masses. For most people Labour was the Left. When they became disillusioned, they turned to the electoral alternative that could form a non-Labour government. What is totally fatalistic is to suggest that all this was inevitable. The limited experience of the Greater London Council (GLC), the Sheffield and

9. An excellent discussion of Wilson's offensive against the National Union of Seamen and his use of the security services against trade unionists is contained in E.P. Thompson, 'Yesterday's Manikin', in *Writings By Candlelight*, London 1980.

Liverpool City Councils indicate that it *is* possible to win support for a radical alternative to both Thatcherism and souped-up Labourism. What is true for a city is equally, if not more, the case for the country as a whole. The fact that it has never been seriously attempted is much more an indictment of Messrs MacDonald, Attlee, Wilson and Callaghan than a reflection of an inherent impossibility of implementing socialist policies on this island. It is not necessary to dwell on this theme now as it is one of the main subjects under discussion in the ensuing conversations with Ken Livingstone.

It was the ignominious defeat of Callaghan by the electorate, after he had failed to defeat the public sector unions, that led the large trade unions to back the reformers within the party. The Wembley conference and the constitutional reforms that followed were the result of a concordat between the CLPs and the unions. However temporary this may have been, it succeeded in changing the face of the Labour Party. A crucial factor in this equation was the new Labour left in the CLPs. The left which has emerged in the Labour Party and trade unions over the last decade and a half is a novel phenomenon, not reducible to earlier movements of the base like that associated with Bevanism in the fifties or Cripps in the thirties. Tony Benn became the central spokesperson and leader of this left, but its appearance should, objectively speaking, be ascribed to the politics of the preceding two decades. The prolonged experience of Labour in office produced a widespread scepticism amongst Labour Party members about the whole notion that socialism could be brought nearer just by what Neil Kinnock has referred to as 'repeated parliamentary victories.'[10] In other words, without Labour governments being constrained – both by extra-

10. In a letter to *The Guardian* (25 November 1981), arguing my inadmissibility as a member of the Labour Party.

parliamentary mobilizations and by constitutional accountability – to carry out party policy. As the contradictions of the
capitalist order in Britain have grown more intractable and
potentially explosive, the Labour Party itself has become the
arena of an intensely antagonistic struggle between labour
and capital. Electoral considerations, as always, are currently
exerting a powerful pressure for unity in the face of the
Tories and the Alliance, but there are good grounds for
scepticism concerning the possibility of a durable 'truce'
between right and left in the Labour Party, at the present
stage of its crisis. What is at stake is the very future of Labour
as a political party.

A structural feature of the Labourist coalition has been an
effective domination of the Party by the Right. Clause Four
may have been kept in the Constitution, but the reality of
Labour has been an effective acceptance not just of capitalism as a system, but by and large of capitalist priorities,
irrespective of the subjective aspirations of the membership.
The capitalist agencies inside the PLP would rather destroy
the party as a governmental candidate than implement some
of the policies recently endorsed by Party conference.
Whereas in the old days Gaitskell could threaten to 'fight,
fight and fight again' to defeat unilateralism and actually win,
the best Kinnock can really hope for is a dilution of the
policy, to be achieved by some calculated ambiguity that will
satisfy nobody. In sum, the internal contradictions within
the Party have intensified to a point where one question
refuses to go away. It is, quite simply, what kind of party will
there be after the dust has settled? This question, especially
at times like the present, is banished to the innermost
recesses of the CLPs' sub-conscious, but it comes immediately to the fore when Hattersely defends wage restraint,
Shore ascribes equal blame to 'both sides in the miners'
dispute', Kaufman is incapable of taking the offensive
against police excesses during the same dispute, and the

Labour Front Bench is berated by Edward Heath for failing to put up a stiffer resistance to the Tories on the issue of abolishing elections in London. If you add to all this the fact that half the Parliamentary Labour Party absented itself from Parliament when the Bill to abolish the GLC and the metropolitan county elections was first put to the vote, it is difficult to accept the view that the installation of the new leadership has fired Right and Centre Labour MPs with a new dynamism. Old questions are very much at the front of their minds. The fudging of political/organizational issues in order to restore the *status quo ante* is thus a line which commands little support. The hard Right want bloodletting and a purge. This view was expressed most clearly by Peter Kellner, the Political Editor of the *New Statesman*, on television's *London Programme* in 1982. Kellner advised Labour's National Executive Committee to disband a dozen or more Labour Parties in London and assert its authority. This was a bit like the American officer during the Vietnam war who told journalists that the only way to save a particular village was by destroying it completely. This view is still held by the Stabians* on the NEC, and arch-Stabian John Golding is now Kinnock's special adviser on 'organizational problems'.[11] Golding would, one presumes, like every Labour Party to be run like his own: a family mafia, in which new members are actively discouraged. The problem is that such hopes cannot

---

* **Stabian** *a.* **1.** (by political inclination) Fabian, interested in power rather than socialism. **2.** (preferred organizational methods) Stalinist, exhibiting utter contempt for democratic norms and procedures. Hostile to spontaneity. **Synonym:** authoritarian.

11. The Stabian offensive reached a peak after Benn's defeat in the Deputy Leadership campaign. The Stabians utilized Foot's weakness to destabilize Peter Tatchell's candidature in Bermondsey. John Golding, then a member of the NEC, played a central part in this fiasco. Tatchell's sexual orientation was utilized as an excuse to attack his politics. Two members of the Shadow Cabinet, whose sexual orientation was similar, were left unmolested by Golding because they shared his Stabian politics. The major responsibility for allowing the Stabians to destroy Tatchell, however, lay with Foot and his Prince of Wales, Neil Kinnock.

be easily fulfilled. On the political level, vying with the SDP for the political mantle of Wilson or Callaghan (or Crosland or Gaitskell) does not offer a convincing perspective for the Labour Party's future. On the organizational level any serious purge would directly affect *at least* fifty per cent of local parties, and antagonize another twenty per cent, without being all that useful electorally. It would merely lend credence to SDP allegations that Labour's well is too deeply poisoned for any water to be drawn from its recesses.

This brings us back to the real significance of the fight to democratize the Labour Party. The domination by the PLP and the block vote, and the enormous powers of the party leader and cabinet, have been the strongest arguments for regarding the Party as structurally incapable of ever being anything other than a top-heavy Labourist monstrosity. Only huge pressures from the outside have produced certain fissures in what appeared as an impregnable edifice. Even the relatively modest changes already achieved have shaken the whole structure and raised fundamental questions about the relationship between unions, party and parliamentary representatives.

The problem of how to ensure that party representatives in parliament do in fact act as *party* representatives is, of course, as old as the first appearance of social-democrat deputies in bourgeois assemblies at the end of the last century (and lay at the root of the split with the ILP in 1929–31). It is only in a country like Britain, where parliament is a potent ideological totem, that large numbers of Labour MPs could be found calmly arguing that they should not be accountable at all to the party, but rather to their 'consciences' or to the electorate as a whole (i.e. nobody). It is only here that a former Labour Prime Minister (Callaghan) could seriously canvass the idea of the PLP formally seceding from the Labour Party, thus taking one back to the days of oligarchic rule and rotten boroughs, before universal suffrage and mass political parties had begun to articulate sectional or class interests on a national scale. The process of reselection of MPs is a far cry from the revocability which was inscribed in the platform of the Paris Commune, but it has already begun to act as a factor of demystification and to pose questions of power within the Labour Party. It is not sufficient simply to look at the small number of MPs who have been de-selected. This is a fact well explained by Livingstone, but what is undeniable is that re-selection reduces the number of professional careerists in the PLP and undercuts the entire mechanism whereby the PLP and Labour Governments operate as agencies of capital inside the Labour movement. This explains the hysterical reaction of ruling-class opinion to the whole notion of accountability of Labour MPs to the Party.

Likewise, although the institution of an electoral college to choose the party leader was in itself a reform of limited importance,[12] it did reveal the enormously undemocratic structures of most unions and posed in an acute form the whole relationship of the Labour Party to the trade unions. The PLP right wing and the media have raised the issue of lack of democracy in the unions as part of their battle against Benn. The Conservative Party pledged during the elections to push through a fundamental 'reform' in order to enable individual trades unionists to determine for themselves whether or not they wished to be members of the Labour Party. In fact they stated clearly that they would introduce a system whereby union members wishing to join Labour would have to opt in by paying the levy rather than opting

12. Ths Swedish sociologist, Göran Therborn, criticized the prevailing parliamentary mysticism in Britain in 'Britian Left Out', *New Socialist*, No. 17, May–June 1984. He wrote: 'In virtually all other member parties of the Socialist International, the party leader is of old elected by the party. Even after Labour's modest constitutional reform, the party's devotion to parliamentary decorum is amazing. For instance, in the recent leadership contests Tony Benn was apparently an impossible candidate even to his own followers, because he was not an MP at the time. In Sweden, the Conservatives elected a new Leader in 1982 who was not a Member of Parliament, and who led his party in the 1982 election without being an MP.'

out as is the case at present. When the triumphant Tories instituted a similar measure after the defeat of the 1926 General Strike, Labour's membership only fell by forty per cent. If it was re-instituted, there can be little doubt that the slump in trade-union membership of the Party would be over fifty per cent.

Once the Labour Party was back in 'safe' hands, however, the Tories uncharacteristically retreated on this issue, but insisted that every trade union affiliated to the Labour Party conduct an internal ballot to ascertain whether a majority of the membership favoured the existence of a political fund. While this may well be a softer option for the Tories, its effects could nonetheless be equally devastating unless a serious effort is made to appeal directly to rank-and-file trade unionists both at their place of work and on housing estates. It is socialists who have a real interest in union democracy, in breaking the grip of the block vote by the immediate institutionalization of proportional voting and direct rank-and-file involvement in decision-making. The block vote has historically been one of the most potent weapons in the hands of the right and strategies based on its utilization by left bureaucrats rather than right bureaucrats have proved particularly barren. A fundamental aim for socialists must be to draw the greatest number of trade unionists into political life. Naturally, there would be no guarantee that, in the first instance, this would mean more support for the Left, but such a change offers the only real hope for a socialist renewal within the Labour movement. In a recent article Jack Jones, the former General Secretary of the T&GWU, has appealed for an end to apathy and a vigorous grassroots campaign against the Tory proposals. He has explicitly stressed the futility of a campaign based on a few mass rallies and the production of countless glossy leaflets. Instead, he writes:

> We face a challenge which can only be met by powerful working organizations at the level of the union district and constituency party.

We will win or lose at that level; and if we are to win, we have to begin right away to consult the people we have there – the shop-stewards and the party workers . . . The campaign in Chesterfield is a good model. We need much the same spirit and strategy, but our forces will be spread over a much wider field. Every shop-steward and every activist must be a propagandist. This has to be a person-to-person campaign, in every workplace. That's where our strength lies – the strength that can break the influence of the media.[13]

Jack Jones is perfectly correct to stress the necessity of a political campaign inside the unions, but the scale of the problem is much larger than is commonly accepted within the Labour Party. What is posed is nothing more or less than re-building Labour within the working class. Mass membership is a useful asset for any political party, as the British Conservatives prove time and time again. In a situation of continuous economic and social crises it is vital. Yet the Labour Party is unique in Western Europe: the bulk of its members are not active in any way in determining the policies or the future of the party. The system of affiliation via the unions reflects the particular birth-processes of British social democracy. The block-vote system is, however, now seen as a charade. A party that cannot modernize itself hardly appears as the most effective candidate for leading Britain into the twenty-first century. Ultimately, of course, Labour should be transformed into a party based on individual members, all possessing the same rights and obligations. This need not prevent any trade union from maintaining a political fund and financing parties which act in its interests, much as large and small firms do in relation to the Tory Party. To start off the process, there are some easy first steps that can be taken to aid the transition. These could include the mandating of trade union delegations in line with the balance of opinions expressed in branches or at conference after all views have been expressed; the breaking-up of the block vote along

13. 'The Unmentionable Menace' by Jack Jones, *ibid*.

proportional lines based on discussion and voting at trade-union conferences; and the establishment of workplace branches of the Labour Party. The present situation is unlikely to be maintained indefinitely, and socialists have everything to gain in arguing for a fundamental transformation of party structures. While there is no acceptable model of relations between a mass party based on the working class and the trade unions, there are some lessons to be learnt from the functioning of the Swedish and Austrian parties in terms of membership and diffusion of political culture. The Austrian party has an individual membership of 700,000 (considerably larger than Labour's) in a country whose population is a little above 7 million. This provides it with a solid material basis for developing its own press and, on certain key issues, challenging the hegemony of the blatantly bourgeois sections of the media.

One does not want to be misunderstood. The historic bond between the Labour Party and its union creators and pay-masters is a positive one. A simple severance would represent a massive regression. It provides a certain class restraint on the career politicians adorning Labour's front bench – which makes the implementation of wholesale austerity measures far more difficult, as Wilson discovered in 1971 and Callaghan in 1978. The present Labour–trade union link is infinitely preferable to the US model of politics, which David Owen and the SDP represent now in a fairly crystallized form. On the other hand, as I have already indicated, there are a number of socialist and communist parties which are linked to unions, without sacrificing the determination of policy and programme by their members. What has to be rejected is the *existing form and structure* of the relationship: the anti-democratic farce whereby Labour's own House of Lords, in the shape of largely unaccountable union general secretaries often elected for life, cast millions of votes at Labour Party conferences (some 90 per cent of the total) in the name of an arbitrarily fixed number of 'members', affiliated at a fraction of the individual member's dues, who, in not a few cases, may actually vote Conservative or SDP. Labour is the only political party in the West with members who vote for its opponents. Surely the very least that is required from the member of any political party is that s/he votes for that party in local or national elections. This fact alone should impel Labour party members to fight for a new form of relationship involving greater active participation of trade-unionists in the Labour Party.

The real problem is not so much the isolation of socialists from the 'broader movement'. What is really at stake is the declining power of socialism as an alternative even to a capitalist system in deep crisis. The 'broad movement' or the working class, which, old and new, still constitutes a large natural majority of the population, has been isolated since 1945 from socialism. This is the heart of the paradox. The working class today remains qualitatively stronger than it was in the late twenties and thirties, but it is qualitatively weaker in relation to a socialist culture. This suggests a different set of remedies than those being prescribed by the fashion-conscious editors of *Marxism Today*. What are the reasons for the existing ideological vacuum? They are varied, but inter-relate in their key aspects with two crucial experiences at home and abroad.

The first is, of course, that we have now had seven Labour Governments in office since the formation of the Labour Party. The first two were minority administrations, the second of which led to a split in the party and a lengthy period of national conservatism. The next two were based on parliamentary majorities which reflected a significantly high popular vote. What followed in the mid-sixties and seventies was (a) 1964: Labour in office with a tiny overall majority of three; (b) 1966: a mini-landslide and a Labour majority of seventy; (c) 1974: two successive Labour Governments with the lowest percentage of the popular vote and dependent for survival on Nationalist and Ulster Unionist MPs. 1924–1974: it was almost as if the Labourist wheel had moved a full circle over those fifty years. The question that arises is this: did any one of the majority Labour Governments offer any serious challenge to the fundamental political or economic coordinates of the British bourgeoisie? Was *socialism* in any shape or form *ever* fought for by Labour in office? The tragedy lies in the fact that millions equated socialism with Labourist experiences that tarnished its appeal. That is one important reason why socialism is not popular today. In fact the entire experience of Labour in office had a profound effect on party ideology. Its political vocabulary underwent a major transformation at the level of the leadership. Note, for instance, the following words, written by the leader of the Labour Party in 1920:

> If bankruptcy ends the present order in disaster and disgrace, if the meanness of mind of our politicians who for momentary triumphs degrade public life and mislead the country like demagogues and charlatans until Parliament has forfeited respect and neither persons nor institutions wield moral or political authority, if prices of commodities keep high and life becomes harder, if we continue to be made the prey of profiteers and plunderers and the evidences of their illgotten gains are to be flaunted in the face of the distressed people, if the mind of the mass is the subject of daily misrepresentation in a contemptible press, and if the desire of the best thought of democracy to find expression and to be consulted as a responsible authority is thwarted by tricksters and cheap jacks, then Labour troubles will become chronic, restlessness will defy reason, anarchy will spread, and social cohesion will be destroyed. Then also the duty of Socialists will be clear. That will be the friction that causes revolution, that will be the hindrance which makes ideas explosive. The Socialists alone can then save the State, and a decisive act of commanding will will be required to do it. It may be a minority that will have to act, but, in this process of creating revolutionary conditions, the majority will have been deprived of its authority, of its intelligence, of its defences, of justice.[14]

14. Bernard Barker, ed., *Ramsay MacDonald's Political Writings*, London 1972.

What is all this? 'A decisive act of commanding will'? 'A minority that will have to act'? The author of this 'ultra-left' anti-parliamentarism is Ramsay MacDonald. Compare this with the mealy-mouthed utterances of Michael Foot when he denounced Peter Tatchell's extremely mild article in *London Labour Briefing*. Recall the same Foot's pathetic parliamentary cretinism in two successive issues of *The Observer* (10 and 17 January 1982), and one gets a fairly precise idea of the shift that has occurred over the last fifty years.

During the 1983 election campaign, Labour's official leaders did not mention capitalism in relation to the economic crisis. Benn and Livingstone did so, and with good effect. They have attempted to popularize socialism, but they remain recent and remarkable exceptions to the general rule.[15] Given all this, it is hardly surprising that socialist policies are not *immediate* crowd-pleasers. Only when they are argued and fought for consistently does it become possible to defeat the capitalist consensus. This is what the peddlars of defeatism do not appreciate. This is what Hobsbawm appears to disregard completely in his desperation to return to a discredited consensus. One sometimes gets the feeling that all those who talk about socialism being unattainable or a remote possibility or whatever, are, in reality, signalling something else. Socialism, for them, is no longer particularly desirable. In which case, it would be far better to drop the pretence and settle down for one of the different capitalist options currently on sale.

There have been, in recent decades, only two occasions on which a successful transformation in East or West could have had a dramatic result in transforming mass consciousness throughout the European continent. The first was the embryonic political revolution that erupted in Prague in 1968. Dubcek's experiment in Czechoslovakia could well have led

15. Eric Heffer is, of course, another exception. In his manifesto for the Labour leadership contest he spelt out clearly the link between capitalism and the crisis.

to, a society without capitalism, but with more real and participatory democracy than exists in the West. The men in the Kremlin, however, were fearful that the pluralist virus might contaminate their own heartlands and become a pole of attraction for citizens and comrades elsewhere in the East. They moved rapidly to extinguish all the hopes that had been aroused. The second instance was, in a way, even more dramatic and pregnant with possibility. The overthrow of the Portuguese dictatorship in 1974 brought a Western European country closer to socialist revolution than at any time since Anglo-American imperialism crushed the Greek resistance after World War Two. If Prague had been overwhelmed by the actual arrival of Brezhnev's tanks, Lisbon was to be lost by 'tankist' conceptions of socialism. The Brezhnevite Portuguese Communist Party, flanked on its left by an assortment of far-left groups, failed to understand the combination of *socialist democracy*. The combined forces of the Portuguese Left were outmanoeuvered and outflanked by Mario Soares, a social-democrat sponsored by the CIA and the right-wing of German social democracy. Soares's demagogy scaled amazing heights as he attacked capitalism in an idiom that would make Messrs Foot, Kinnock, Hobsbawm and Crick wince in agony. In fact Soares reconstructed the Socialist Party by speaking a militant language, itself an indication of the mood among the Portuguese working class. Hence the following passage from the SP manifesto:

> The Socialist Party fights the capitalist system and bourgeois domination . . . The SP is implementing a new conception of life that can only be brought about by the construction of workers power . . . The struggle against fascism and colonialism will only be achieved by the destruction of capitalist society and the construction of socialism . . . The SP refutes those who say they are social-democrats but continue to preserve the *status quo*, the structures of capitalism and the interests of imperialism.

It was Soares's ability to appropriate the banners of *both* socialism and democracy that enabled him to leap over the Portuguese CP and the far-left, who were infatuated with putschist notions and lacked a real strategy for winning over the majority of workers and peasants in the South as well as the North. Today Soares is an ardent admirer of Margaret Thatcher and on the extreme right of European social-democracy. The defeat of the Portuguese revolution in November 1975 ended the first phase of the stormy and tempestuous period that had begun in 1968 and had put socialism, as a feasible prospect, back on the agenda for Western Europe.[16]

The setbacks in Prague and Lisbon, the experiences of the Wilson/Callaghan governments in Britain, the Brandt/ Schmidt years in the Federal Republic of Germany, the cold-war 'socialism' of François Mitterrand, the froth-ridden Gonzalez exercises in Spain, the impotent manoeuvring of the PCI in Italy, have all left their mark on the consciousness of millions of workers. There are undoubted dangers in the present situation, but all is by no means lost. There are already some clear signs of a new reawakening. West Germany and Britain, the two countries where social-democratic experiments in managing capitalism led to the victory of the Right, share certain features in common: large peace movements, a growth of working-class combativity against unemployment (miners in Britain, metal workers in Germany), emergence of the Greens and their interrelation-ship with the SPD and the birth of the new Labour Left. It is the latter which is the concern of this small book.

In a lengthy article in March 1982, Quintin Hoare and myself put forward an analysis which argued that socialists should join and regroup within the Labour Party. We argued that the socialist project would receive a tremendous boost if

16. See Tariq Ali, '1968 And After', London 1978. There is a more detailed discussion of this problem in Tariq Ali, ed., *The Stalinist Legacy*, 1984, forth-coming.

Labour were to be refounded, at some future stage, as a socialist party and that this was not a utopian scheme, but a practical possibility which would be brought nearer if sectarianism was eschewed and socialists outside Labour linked arms anew with their comrades fighting for change within the Party. Since our theses were subjected to much criticism and since, it could be argued, the ascent to power within Labour of a 'dream-ticket' has made any prospect of further change a distant one, it is worth recalling our argument in some detail, especially in relation to the basic choices facing the Labour Party:

> There are three basic ways forward being prospected by sections of the existing Labour leadership, and which of them prevails is not a matter of indifference to socialists. The first, advocated by the Manifesto Group and the trade-union right, is to fight, fight and fight again to create a Mark II SDP. This requires not merely isolating Benn, but decisively defeating his base in party and unions alike. This can now only be achieved after the next general election – perhaps by blaming the left for defeat, as a prelude to a determined purge. Once the SDP/Liberals in their turn prove unable to solve the crisis, in this Manifesto scenario, there would once again be a cleansed and purified Labour Party on offer to the ruling class, in the role of coalition partner if not of sole governmental candidate.
>
> The second option, favoured by Foot and the bulk probably of the union leadership, is to strive to restore the Grand Old Party as before. It involves uniting with the right against the left, but at the same time restraining it at least until after the next election. It involves fudging over unwelcome conference policies and minimizing the practical effect of recent constitutional changes, rather than defeating and reversing them as the right would like. It is no doubt at present more hostile than the right to any ideas of coalition in the future, though this is unlikely to survive the harsh test of post-electoral reality. It is more wedded to the traditional relationship between party and unions – though union leaders themselves can be assumed to have a fundamentally pragmatic attitude on this question. At bottom, this option is a short-term one, unlikely to survive either Foot himself or the next general election. Its basic dilemma has been thrown into harsh light by its equivocations on the question of a purge. There has been constant and mounting pressure from the PLP right, sections of the union bureaucracy and the

media for a thorough-going purge of the Labour Party, to turn it into a tame instrument of bourgeois hegemony in the working class. The scope of what is envisaged is perhaps indicated by the habitual use of the designation 'hard left', even in the so-called quality press, to denote Benn and his co-thinkers in parliament or Livingstone and his colleagues on the GLC. Foot and his supporters from the old Tribune left have shown themselves increasingly willing and indeed anxious to comply, in order to conciliate the right and please a supposedly irredeemably anti-socialist electorate. However, they have also been forced to realize that there are enormous obstacles to carrying through any such purge, without its becoming a fatal split – fatal to the whole Foot project, that is – given the overwhelming leftward orientation of the constituency parties; the degree of militant consciousness among trade-union activists who can no longer so easily be ignored by authoritarian general secretaries; and the significant left minority that exists within the union leadership and even within the PLP (as shown by the 66 votes for Benn in the shadow cabinet elections, against Foot's express recommendation). The right when it says 'purge', really means 'split'. Insofar as Foot and his advisers believe the former is possible without the latter, this is part of their more general illusion that the crisis (external and internal) can be willed away and the old status quo conjured back into existence. This illusion is fated to be dispelled sooner rather than later.

The third option, adumbrated at least tendentially by Benn, is to create a New Model Labour Party. Unable to restore bourgeois confidence in it as a reliable pillar of the governmental system, under constant attack from the media, Labour would seek to restore its links with a battered working-class base, offering a programme which would outrage – even if not challenge fundamentally – the capitalist class. Such a perspective would necessitate building Labour as a mass, socialist party by drawing rank-and-file union activists into effective political participation, changing the existing style of political work and consolidating the electoral reforms by transforming the intrinsically anti-democratic block vote and devoting more time and energy to programmatic elaboration of a broadly socialist character. The launching of a popular socialist weekly to argue the positions of the left within a national political arena would then become a crucial necessity.[17]

Shortly after that article was written an ugly incubus in the

17. Tariq Ali and Quintin Hoare, 'Socialists and the Crisis of Labourism', *New Left Review* 132, March – April 1982.

shape of the war over the Falklands engulfed British politics. Labour's Front Bench capitulated to a depraved jingoism, with Foot scarcely being able to conceal his admiration for the Iron Lady. Labour's policies, supposedly commited to peace, were thus deprived of any real credibility. It was the failure of the Foot–Healey–Kinnock team to oppose the Falklands aventure that helped to shore up the image of the Conservative Prime Minister as defiant and unbeatable. This, much more than the internal divisions in the party, made a second Thatcher victory virtually inevitable. As the real Admirals and Generals dominated the media, so the leaders of the Labour Party and the SDP put on their fancy-dress cockades and their peaked caps to discuss the pros and cons of the murderous manoeuvres in the South Atlantic. The language was that of *Boys' Own*. 'If only it had been handled like I handled the confrontation with Indonesia', roared General Healey. 'No, no!' screeched Admiral Owen, 'if a few gunboats had been despatched as happened when I was Foreign Secretary none of this would have happened.' In this atmosphere it was hardly surprising that the lower orders in Fleet Street had a field day. Tony Benn and the handful of Labour MPs who opposed the war were denounced as traitors, scum. With the political atmosphere so heavily polluted Thatcher swept to an easy victory at the polls.

The point is that a united Labour opposition could, at the very least, have given hope and heart to a minority that was prepared to be mobilized for peace, but found no political party providing a lead.[18] A vigorous opposition might also have acted as a restraint on Thatcher and the war cabinet, possibly even preventing the wanton murder of the Argentinian sailors aboard the *Belgrano*.

On this question as well, Eric Hobsbawm retreated yet

18. For a spirited attack on the war and the atmosphere that prevailed, see Anthony Barnett's *Iron Brittania*, London 1981.

further. In 'Falklands Fallout' (*Marxism Today*, January 1983) he advised the Left not to let Thatcher monopolize patriotism and jingoism. He recalled that the Chartists of old were also great patriots, whose chauvinism was concealed by their militancy. Hobsbawm advocated the combination of class struggle and nationalism and stated that 'when the two go together in harness, they multiply not only the force of the working class but its capacity to place itself at the head of a broad coalition for social change, and they even give it the possibility of wresting hegemony from the class enemy.' Thus, on the only recent occasion where he has talked about class power, it has been done in the name of the Union Jack. Hobsbawm also returned to the Popular Front period and claimed that the French Left had 'tried to conquer, capture and recapture both the tricolour and Joan of Arc and to some extent it succeeded.' He didn't specify the extent. Did success lie in allowing the Spanish Republic to be destroyed while Blum proclaimed 'non-intervention'? Or perhaps it was the incredible resistance mounted to prevent the Nazi occupation of France. Or then again it could have been the enormous successes of Thorez after the war, just prior to the PCF being unceremoniously booted out of the government by de Gaulle. Joan of Arc must have fled to Moscow!

A more dangerous tendency is the presentation of an extremely selective and partial version of history. Chartism contained a number of currents and cannot be categorized as jingoist without serious qualifications. But why does a historian of Hobsbawm's calibre stop at the Chartists? Why not go a bit further back in history. Were there not sizeable working-class movements in solidarity with the French Revolution? Is it not the case that in 1798, when Britain was in a state of war with France (a slightly more serious business than the Falklands), there were three daily papers in London, *Morning Chronicle*, *Morning Post* and *The Courier*, which were strongly critical of the Government and its foreign policy. Why did the Foreign Office feel the urge to distribute its own newssheet in the shape of Canning's *Anti-Jacobin*? Why did Edmund Burke's *Reflections on the French Revolution* sell only 30,000 copies while Thomas Paine's *Rights of Man* sold 1,500,000? Who was reading Paine and where? The 'left-of-centre middle-classes'? The university-educated rationalists? I fear not. It was the plebeians who devoured Jacobin propaganda, necessitating censorship and repression. That is a far more honourable tradition than the later displays of jingoism. Why should the left stop at appropriating patriotism from the chauvinists? Surely racism and sexism are equally strong currents. Should we then have socialist variants of the same? Where will it all end, Professor Hobsbawm?

It was this defeatist mood that brought electoral defeat for Labour in 1983. Michael Foot resigned as Leader. Tony Benn had been denied a safe seat in Bristol (thanks to Stabian machinations in Walworth Road) and he suffered a tragic defeat. The trade-union leaders wanted a painless accession. Neil Kinnock had leapt to fame by offering his conscience on a platter to the Labour Right and the media establishment and ensuring Benn's defeat as Deputy Leader in 1981. He now coolly stepped into place and was duly elected Leader of the Labour Party. For once the PLP, the CLPs, the unions and the consensus merchants of the media were in complete accord. Shell-shocked by defeat, the Labour Party clung in desperation to men of straw. The only discordant note was struck by Richard Gott, the Features Editor of *The Guardian*. In a savage polemic against Kinnersley/Hattock, Gott simultaneously gave voice to the feeling of many Labour activists by his impassioned defence of Benn and Livingstone. Re-read today, long after the euphoria of the 1983 Brighton Conference, Gott's text (which his newspaper appropriately published on a page reserved for outsiders) remains a powerful and prescient plea for a radical, socialist party in this country.[19]

The election of Kinnock/Hattersley has resulted in a truce on the innerparty front. This is likely to last till the next general election. No section of the Labour Party wants to be held responsible for paving the way for a Thatcher hat-trick. Moreover, as both Benn and Livingstone have pointed out on various occasions, Kinnock is the first leader of the Party to be elected under the new system and is, as a consequence, unchallengeable until 1988. All this is perfectly comprehensible within the framework of electoral politics, but there are two additional factors that need to be borne in mind. First is the actual level of resistance to the Tories by the working class itself. The level of mobilization by the miners during the 1984 miners' strike has been a remarkable demonstration of class solidarity by a substantial section of the National Union of Mineworkers. The overkill response of the State testified to the amazing degree of militancy and the large numbers involved in the strike itself. If industrial struggles were to develop an upward curve, there would be a growing pressure for the Labour Front Bench to play a more active role in support of the same.

Secondly, there is a process of replenishment of members taking place. The local resistance to the Tories symbolized by the Greater London Council, Sheffield, Liverpool and, possibly, Manchester, is a reflection of the changing political composition of the CLPs. Compare the new model Labour councillors to the Old Corruption of yesterday and a picture emerges of what is taking place, albeit unevenly, throughout the country. This is an inevitable process, for every political party confronts the iron laws of

19. Richard Gott, 'Tony and Ken, the Natural Leaders that Labour needs but Can't Have', *The Guardian*, 17 June 1984. Reprinted as Appendix One below.

biology. Old members begin to die. New ones take their place. Where will they come from? In the case of Labour there is now little room for doubt that many of those who left the Party during the years of the locust (Wilson in power) began to return in the mid-seventies. Thus the radicalization of 1968 found a partial base inside the Labour Party. This is not a homogeneous social layer. Nor is it monolithic, but it is extremely distrustful of traditional Labourism.

The new influx is also implacably hostile to the corrupt corporatism of the old-style Labour councils, which did so much to alienate working people from the Labour Party. They could be observed in all their gory crookedness throughout the sixties and the seventies: Tyneside, the Midlands, the London boroughs of Islington, Tower Hamlets and Bermondsey were the most grotesque specimens of localized Labourism. How could Labour have ever lost Liverpool to the gimmickry of a reactionary wing of native Liberalism? The answer lies in decaying services, neglected housing estates, an alienated working population. This and much worse was the real legacy of the right-wing Labour mafias who ran the traditional strongholds of the working class. The fact that the social origins of many of these corrupt councillors lay in the same class should not be a matter of great surprise. In such situations it is the primacy of politics that really matters. The people who served on Clay Cross Council in Derbyshire during the early seventies were also workers. Their roots were in the local community, and they never sought to break loose on an individualist get-rich-quick racket. At the same time as the Clay Cross councillors were challenging the Heath government, hardly a week went by in South Wales without a Labour councillor being brought to trial on charges of corruption. Why is it that the crooks invariably belonged to the hard right of the Labour Party? An accident? A freak occurrence? Or something more? A reflection, in fact, of the total failure of Labourism to challenge the rule of capital in any significant way. These local processes were also repeated on a national level during and after Labour's years in office. Many of yesterday's Labour Cabinet ministers found safe havens in the heart of capitalism, where they used their dubious talents to attack the very people who had elected them to office. The last Treasurer of the Labour Party, Eric Varley (former Member for Chesterfield), is merely the latest in a long line of 'City-roaders'. The scandals associated with Wilson's inner circle during the twilight years of his Prime Ministership were, in effect, concealed from the full gaze of the public by a conformist media and the curious legal system that operates in this country. Yet they could not hide the fact that some of the shady businessmen friends of the former Prime Minister ended up in prison or committing suicide to avoid further investigation.[20] Such activities were not merely remote from socialism, they had nothing to do even with the self-proclaimed modernist urges defended by Wilson during his election campaigns.

It is this entire tradition of right-wing politics, behind-the-scenes deals with political enemies, that is under threat. The press attacks on Livingstone, Blunkett, Hatton (or on Margaret Hodge and Hilda Kean, who lead the Labour councils in Islington and Hackney) are motivated by a desire to prevent any change at all costs. It is dustbin-journalism with a vengeance, but it also brings to light the role of the press which boasts of standing above the gutter. The *Daily Mirror* has published some extremely savage attacks on Livingstone and the GLC regime. *The Guardian*'s 'political staff' have not been much better. In short, there is not a single Fleet Street paper which has actively backed the attempt to sweep the old muck out of the stench-ridden

20. There is an evocative account of this in Peter Tatchell, *The Battle for Bermondsey*, London 1983.

Labourist stables. In fact when activists in the Liberal Party have attempted to follow the model of the new Labour Left, they have been subjected to ringing denunciations by *Guardian* columnists.[21] It is hardly surprising that in a country like Britain where ideology plays such a crucial role in preserving the stability of the system, the media should be so totally submissive to the needs of the ruling Establishment. The net result of this is to make the British press the worst and most conformist in those parts of the world where there are no formal restrictions on press freedom. It is difficult to imagine any British newspaper campaigning against a Government as the *Washington Post* did against Nixon and Watergate. The *Frankfurter Rundschau* consistently publishes a far greater range of opinions than *The Guardian*. Austria and Sweden boast a vigorous and critical social-democratic press, which competes directly with capitalist newspapers. One can also, without much difficulty, concur with Salman Rushdie's view that *The Telegraph* (published daily in Calcutta) is infinitely superior to any Fleet Street daily. We could add to this the remarkable Mexican daily *Uno mas Uno*, which also has no equivalent in this country. This reliance by traditional Labourism on the existing Fleet Street productions was not simply misplaced, but totally counter-productive. The *Mirror* bosses had, in 1981, agreed informally that if Tony Benn had been elected Deputy Leader of the Labour Party, they would not call for a vote for Labour in the ensuing general election.

Where does all this leave us in relation to the future of the Labour Party? Can the present half-way house continue indefinitely? I think not. It may be politic for Labour's socialist politicians to lie low for a while and say little to disturb the reigning orthodoxy. Time is, after all, on their side. What is really needed, however, is a meaningful

21. See Appendix Two below.

socialist programme for the Labour Party, which aims to win over a majority of working people to socialist policies. Even the necessarily limited projects of the radical local governments in London, Sheffield and Liverpool indicate the possibilities of unfreezing politics on a national level. But what about the 'broad church'? This was always an utterly bogus notion, utilized by Wilson to assure a spurious unity behind his particular brand of Labourism. The 'broad church' concept only has meaning if the Right are in complete control. The formation of the SDP has weakened the Right immeasurably and there will be further defections if Labour does not win an overall majority in 1988. Yet even within its own terms a 'broad church' implies some agreement on principle. There are, after all, many broad churches within Christendom: Catholic, Protestant, Greek Orthodox, Methodist, Russian Orthodox, etc. I agree with Arthur Scargill in favouring a socialist 'broad church', but a 'church' which includes both the followers of capital and those who wish to replace it with a different economic structure? The tension will have to be resolved, and until it is the problems will not disappear. They are not the product of the personalities of Benn or Livingstone, but rather manifestations of the objective processes which are reshaping British politics. The Falklands Freeze is over and politics will become relevant again.

Ken Livingstone is a product of the changes that have already taken place in the Labour Party. His first biographer, John Carvel, has produced an extremely fair volume in *Citizen Ken*, but his failure to see Livingstone as first and foremost a militant socialist derives from his lack of an apparatus necessary to make that judgement. Livingstone's right-wing opponents claim that he is an opportunist simply using the Left to climb up the ladder. Surely this should be something close to their own hearts, and if they believe themselves they should be behind Livingstone!

In fact Livingstone is the most gifted representative of the new Labour Left. He speaks a different language from the careerist Labour politicians who end up in the House of Lords after having preached the virtues of class-collaboration, incomes policies, subordination to NATO and a blind acceptance of the social and sexual *status quo*.[22] Livingstone is the first Labour politician since Herbert Morrison to utilize County Hall as a political power base from which to influence the direction of Labour on a national level. Like Morrison, he is a product of the South London working class, but unlike him he has moved towards militant socialism rather than in the opposite direction. Morrison had a left-wing past. He was a member of Hyndman's Social Democratic Federation, well-versed in the Marxist classics (he was born four years after Marx's death) and street-meetings, before moving straight to the Centre of the Labour Party.

Livingstone, on the other hand, spent his youth on what, to most radicals of his own generation, was the other side of the barricades from the Marxist left. His centre of gravity has always been the nitty-gritty of practical labour movement politics. His target is undeniably power within the existing institutions of the Labour Movement, their transformation and then an assault on the citadels of economic power in capitalist Britain. Media-people would be foolish to ignore Livingstone's strong committment to socialism. He was radicalized by his study of anthropology, the emergence of the women's movement and the anti-imperialist struggles of the sixties. His understanding of sexual politics and his defence of gay rights and sexual liberation has enraged every establishment in the country. Yet he has not retreated one

22. The media, unsurprisingly, present the anti-NATO lobby as the voice of the 'hard left'. A respected Labour patriarch, the late G.D.H. Cole, in his last article 'Next Steps in Foreign Policy', regarded a withdrawal from NATO and all cold-war alliances as the touchstone of a socialist foreign policy. See *The New Reasoner*, Summer 1958, for a detailed exposition of his views. Kinnock and Hattersley, in contrast, are staunch men of NATO.

inch. Surely this is an unusual record for a prominent Labour politician, and is an indication of his toughness once he is committed to a cause.

Yet, I'm afraid, he will have to plough through some of the socialist classics sooner or later, and *not* for any moral reasons. He will find this crucial for formulating an alternative socialist strategy for Britain and challenging existing orthodoxies. When Callaghan became Chancellor of the Exchequer, he had special tutorials in economics at Nuffield College, Oxford. Other Cabinet ministers were simply educated by 'their' civil servants. Livingstone will, I'm sure, discover that a socialist self-education is the only solution.

The post-1979 period has made two basic truths abundantly clear. The days of old SDP-style reformism, exemplified by Bevin, Morrison, Wilson, Callaghan, Healey, Hattersley are over, but so are all the dreams which kept many of us high during the sixties and seventies, when we visualized bypassing the established institutions of the Labour Movement in one big leap. The alliances which need to be fought for and brought about are between the new breed of socialist politicians exemplified by Livingstone and the generation of Marxists brought up on the writings of Miliband, Mandel and Anderson. Perhaps the attempt to reconstruct Labour along socialist lines will come to grief, as similar efforts did in the past. It would be foolish to become as dogmatic about this possibility as one was over its polar opposite in 1968 and after. What can be said with certainty is that a serious, socialist project in Britain requires a fusion of the theoretical reach and grasp of a wide layer of Marxists with the practical skills, abilities and courage of leaders able to communicate with millions such as Benn, Scargill and Livingstone.

The ensuing conversations with Livingstone cover many aspects of the politics that symbolize the new Labour left. Only an unredeemable sectarian could argue that the emergence of this left is a roadblock on the path to socialism. If anything, it represents an element of hope in an otherwise gloomy situation. The real problem is this: if a future Labour government or a consensual Coalition were to behave like its predecessors, the consequences would be disastrous, for the proponents of a more authoritarian application of capitalist norms are already waiting in the wings and not all of them are in the Conservative Party. It is in order to prevent that option from ever being exercised that we need a socialist Labour Party.

London, 7 June 1984

Part One

Why Labour Lost

Before we discuss the post-electoral situation in Britain and its possible consequences for the Labour Party, I would like to ask you just one 'personal' question. Soon after you were elected Leader of the Greater London Council (GLC), you spoke at a left-wing rally where you shared a platform with Ernest Mandel. Your self-introduction to that particular audience was somewhat unique. You informed us that you had joined the Labour Party in 1968. I was somewhat bemused listening to you, since tens of thousands of us had been leaving the Labour Party in that period. What made you join at that precise moment in time? On the face of it your decision seems virtually inexplicable.

I was interested in politics from the age of eleven in 1956, but it was only an interest. Both my parents were working-class Conservatives, but of the sort who preferred the Tory patricians. They liked Churchill a lot, but grew progressively less fond of every succeeding Tory leader. My mother is now a Bennite! My father's parents died when he was fourteen and he immediately joined the merchant navy as a seaman. The only progressive streak in him was a tolerance towards people of other races. He was strongly anti-racist. While other people in my age-group were already immersed in socialist politics – in and out of all sorts of left-wing organizations – my time was largely spent in the pursuit of natural history. That was my passion at the time. I was active in the breeding of frogs and much more concerned with preserving the species. So, it was a very unusual background.

My shift towards a more active involvement in politics began with the assassination of Kennedy and the election of Wilson, first as Leader of the Labour Party and then as Prime Minister. Prior to that, my involvement in politics had essentially been confined to laughing at Macmillan and Home, whom I found to be terribly boring and dreadful patricians. The election of Wilson suddenly focused my attention on the Labour Party, and I was quite fixed on the idea that this Harold Wilson character was actually going to change things. I made the fatal mistake of believing in Harold Wilson. I still remember trembling with excitement when we won the 1964 elections, but I had still not *joined* the Labour Party. Then in 1966, of course, I was already disillusioned with Wilson. My friends were either anarcho-syndicalists or members of what was then the International Socialists – none of them, incidentally, is currently engaged in any form of politics. But it was through them that I ended up on the big Vietnam demonstrations. For a short period I joined an organization called Solidarity. Is it still going?

Just about . . .

It was *just about* going then! But I didn't play much of a role in its deliberations. I suppose there were three experiences which propelled me towards the Labour Party. Firstly the Unit where I worked – a Cancer Research Unit – had a policy of redundancies to overcome a financial deficit. So, with a couple of other people I organized a branch of ASTMS (Association of Scientific, Technical and Managerial Staffs) and we started to unionize the whole place. Secondly John Fraser, the Labour MP in Norwood where I was living at the time, had a very good position on racism – an issue that mattered a lot to me. His Tory opponent had been a member of the 'Hang Them, Flog Them and Send Them Back Home

Brigade'. (He has, by the way, disappeared into oblivion since he was caught in some embezzlement racket.) Thirdly I got involved in helping American draft resisters, who did not want to fight in Vietnam. I had met some of them while hitch-hiking in Africa. These three circumstances helped me to decide where I was going. It was just so obvious. There was no way in which you were going to build anything without the Labour Party. Perhaps because my interest in politics was geared to psephology and things like that, rather than to pure ideology, it was more obvious to me than to others at the time. The solid attachment of millions of working-class people to the Labour Party meant that it was this party which had to be taken over and changed. So I joined.

The first ward meeting I went to was appalling. I was the only person below pensionable age. This was soon after the Socialist Labour League had been expelled from the Labour Party and the Young Socialists. The International Socialists left soon after. Norwood Labour Party had been filleted and gutted by people giving up in shock and horror and quitting. Three months after joining I found myself on the Executive Committee of the General Management Committee and also chairman and secretary of the local Young Socialists. The latter body had one other member! The first debate we had was on 'In Place of Strife' and we mandated Fraser to oppose it in Parliament. This was in 1969 and I still remember the vote on the GMC. It was 13 to 9. The Labour Party was at its absolute nadir in terms of membership and activists. There has since been a slow build-up, which has been camouflaged by phoney membership statistics for years. The pits for the Labour Party was 1968–69 and we've been witnessing a slow recovery ever since.

Was there some book which influenced you towards socialism?

No. It was all practical things: my workplace involvement,

helping my American friends, and so on. I've never been a theoretician. By the time I reached the stage where I wanted to read more theoretical works, I was already on the Council. That was in 1971, and ever since I've been reading council agendas. It's really terrible. Look around this room. Life is a flurry of paper, much of which I won't have time to read. It's a question of deciding whether they should be filed.

After the 1959 election defeat, when the Party was led by Hugh Gaitskell and the Labour Right, the analysis of the debacle was strangely familiar. It was that the Party's links with the trade unions were a hangover from the past; that Clause Four[1] was an unnecessary encumbrance; and that Labour could only win if it modernized itself on the American pattern (a message Margaret Thatcher repeated during this campaign). It could hardly be argued that Gaitskell had fought a left-wing campaign, or that the Party had been taken over by 'Marxist infiltrators'. The Right failed in its attempt to remove Clause Four from the Constitution, but in practice it never let that bother it in any way. It is almost as if there were an iron law of labourism. When a Labour Opposition fails to win office, there is a rapid drift to the right. It is an iron law, I should add, which is influenced by the magnet of capitalist democracy and the firm limits it has set for British politics. However, the 1983 election defeat is somewhat unique. In the thirties the bulk of the parliamentary Labour leadership had decamped to the Tories and the victory of a so-called 'National Coalition' was almost inevitable. In 1959 you still had an economic boom, albeit in its twilight phase. In 1951 Labour had lost but with a much higher popular vote. This time we've lost in the middle of mass unemployment, with a more radical mani-

1. The new constitution of the Labour Party, largely drafted by Henderson and Webb and adopted at the 1918 Annual Conference, contained 'Clause Four' committing the movement 'To secure for the producers by hand and brain the full fruits of their industry, and the most equitable distribution thereof that may be possible, upon the basis of the common ownership of the means of production and the best obtainable system of popular administration and control of each industry and service.'

festo than in previous years, and against an unashamedly right-wing Tory government. How would you analyse this defeat?
Tribune *has laid all the blame, and emotionally this is understandable, on the 'guilty men' of the Labour Right. Yet it seems to me somehow shallow, simplistic and unconvincing to blame the defeat exclusively on Callaghan, Healey, Shore and Hattersley. Something more is involved, is there not?*

I think there is a fairly inevitable pattern which doesn't operate at the time of a real economic collapse beyond what we are experiencing at the moment. In times of a moderate boom or a bad recession the existence of a social-democratic government does push the Party to the left, as it sees very clearly that the traditional solutions are not working. The overwhelming majority of Party and trade-union activists are not theoreticians: their views are formed through living experiences. They can see why Labour governments aren't working, and this moves them to the left. I believe that this is how Tony Benn ended up on the left. When you have a Tory government like this last one and we suffer a devastating defeat at the polls, there is a tendency to forget previous Labour governments and their policies. Despair aids political amnesia, and even the most ordinary social-democratic prescription appears benign when compared with the Tories. I agree that it is a fairly standard pattern: I remember arguing with Californian activists in the late sixties along similar lines. They were saying it didn't matter if Reagan was elected Governor of California, as the worse things became, the better would be the prospects for radical upheavals. It never works like that.

This time was different. We put forward social-democratic policies, in some instances of a souped-up variety. The difference between our manifesto and that of the SDP was only a matter of degree, especially on the economic policies needed to pull out of the present crisis. The fine print of our manifesto was much more radical, but what the public heard was mainly the interpretations of Shore and Hattersley. The SDP would borrow £8 billion. Shore wanted to borrow £11 billion. It was all deeply unconvincing. Potential Labour voters have a much sharper understanding of the economy than many activists realize. Expressing it in everyday terms rather than the language which activists use, they could see that the weak and watered-down economic policies which Shore presented were simply not going to work. I don't think that the Labour leadership was convinced that they were going to work, and that weakness came through in every public debate with the Tories and the SDP/Liberal Alliance. The package they were offering was a marginally more radical version of what had previously failed under Wilson and Callaghan.

People know that, unless Labour tackles the existing concentration of wealth, funding the programme of good things we wish to do involves tax increases. You could get away with tax increases in 1964 and 1966 after a period in which living standards had risen over the years, but the situation today is radically different. Taxes have gone up under Thatcher, and working-class families know that they simply cannot afford to pay for solving the problems of poverty in contemporary Britain. And they're right. They refuse to accept any more redistribution of wealth among the poor. They were unconvinced by Labour, and many of them (including half of the unemployed) didn't come out to vote. Some did vote Tory, impressed by a 'firm leadership' in striking contrast to our disarray. What this election shows is that a long period is needed to put across arguments before they begin to bear fruit. I don't think that if we had managed to put Tony Benn in command in February or March, the results would have been all that different. Our policies have to be argued for. That is why we need a Leader who spends the bulk of his time not in parliament, but campaigning on how we intend to end unemployment. He should turn up for Question Time, but not spend his nights in the House. Instead the Party should lay on two or three meetings a week throughout the country.

The Working-Class Vote

How do you explain the fact that a plurality of skilled workers (39%) voted for the Tories, whereas only 35% voted Labour. Surely this is the crux of the problem. The ability of the Tories to win a large share of the working-class vote has not yet been seriously analysed or understood. Nottingham today is without a single Labour member of Parliament. It may be unpalatable, but could there be something in the argument that explains the dichotomy in the working-class vote by the fact that skilled workers in employment have not experienced the same reduction in living standards as they did during the last years of the Callaghan regime. This is reflected not just in the Midlands, but also in Greater London. How do you see the working-class Tory voter?

I think that the working-class Tory vote is triggered by a number of interrelated mechanisms. Where the majority are still in work, where you have a skilled working-class community and where they've bought their own homes, they are better off. Those who live in rented accommodation are not better off. I think this is what amplifies working-class conservatism, but its roots are much deeper and probably more profound in Britain than elsewhere in Europe. These relate to the impact of colonialism and imperialism on the formation of working-class consciousness. Our working class grew out of colonialism. The skilled craft unions of the last century benefited enormously from Britain's imperial role. Joseph Chamberlain had a massive base in the working class of the Midlands. This division still colours the modern Labour movement. If you look at the divisions in the TUC, you find that the skilled craft unions that grew out of the Empire are the extreme right of the movement. The Engineers backed

Healey in the struggle for the deputy leadership – the Electricians are virtually in the arms of the SDP.

In these conditions it is hardly surprising that the Falklands War benefited the Tories in working-class communities. Even though a shift to the Tories was discernible before that conflict, the victory itself consolidated the trend. If you look at the local council elections that took place in London during the war, there was an actual swing to Labour in wards with a substantial Irish, black or unskilled working-class community. In areas where there was a more traditional, settled, white working class our vote collapsed by up to a half. In Hornchurch and Hayes the vote crumbled. The same pattern was repeated in the general election. In constituencies like Hackney North and Peckham the Labour vote was very good. Even in London constituencies like Hornsey, Hampstead, Dulwich, Norwood and Westminster North, where black and Irish people live side by side with large numbers of white middle-class professionals, there were swings to Labour. Maybe the racists have all gone off to live in Finchley or Croydon South. Therefore at this election, even though people say that the Falklands War took place a year ago and that voters weren't thinking of the South Atlantic when they voted, I think that deep cultural and political attitudes, going back a hundred years or more, were freshly awakened during the war.

People had watched Britain decline as a superpower ever since the Second World War. When a weaker country then came along, whose armed forces were nowhere near our strength, the mere fact that Britain was able to beat the hell out of it gave a massive boost to the old nationalism and jingoism. Given the Labour Party's appalling record on the Falklands, we weren't particularly helped at the voter's doorstep. It is an interesting contrast with how the Labour Party handled Suez under a right-wing leader – for, after an initial stumble, Gaitskell realized it was lunacy and spoke out loudly against the Expeditionary Force. We still didn't win a majority on the issue, but we did carve out a solid chunk for our position. This time Peter Shore and Michael Foot drifted along in an orgy of jingoism and Blimpery, conceding the crucial ground to the Tories at the very start. Since all three opposition parties backed the Government to the hilt, it was hardly surprising that the country followed suit. Healey's and Kinnock's references to the Falklands War during the closing stages of this campaign were not just belated, but sounded phoney. The time to have opposed was when the war was begun. I think Labour's decision to back Thatcher in the South Atlantic was a crucial error, and we have paid the price. Opposition would not have automatically ensured that we won, but at least we would have countered the prevailing mood and maintained ideological bridgeheads which would have been invaluable later.

Electoral Reform

If we could now turn to another important issue that has emerged from this general election: the thorny problem of electoral reform. One can hardly ignore the fact that Thatcher's 'landslide majority' is based on 30.8% of the total electorate and 42% of the popular vote. In fact the Tory victory was only possible because Britain, uniquely in Europe, has an antiquated 'first-past-the-post system' which distorts the actual vote. It has not been popular on the Left, as Arthur Scargill and myself have discovered over the years, to argue in favour of some form of proportional representation. Within the Labour Party there is great hostility to the idea, largely for pragmatic and opportunist reasons, but surely it is time to re-evaluate the problem. If we had won the election on a minority vote and attempted to implement unilateral nuclear disarmament or to abolish the House of Lords, the outcry would have been heard all the way across the Atlantic. The media would have unleashed a ferocious campaign denying that Labour had a popular mandate, and they would have had the figures on their side. Now, initially Labour might not do so well out of a system of PR, though I can't see how it would do worse. But don't you think that the present electoral system is patently undemocratic? The majority of voters did not vote for the Tories, but we have a Conservative government with a 144-seat majority. Surely this is not simply an anomaly, but an outrage.

In principle I have always been in favour of proportional representation. By this I specifically mean something like the German system, where over half the members of parliament are directly elected, and a topping-up then operates on the basis of the actual votes received by different parties. I would simply insist that the topping-up would have to be of defeated candidates, on the basis of the highest vote downwards. Otherwise you give too much power to the party bureaucracy. I've been in favour of this for years, though I haven't spent too many sleepless nights worrying about the injustices of the British electoral system. I have been more lukewarm since the SDP/Liberal Alliance made it a central plank of their campaign. I am utterly opposed to the Single Transferable Vote which they support – that is not PR, but simply a mechanism for keeping one particular party out of office. The big thing that caused me to lose a lot of enthusiasm for PR was the changing of the German government without a fresh popular mandate. I am in favour of PR, but I am not in favour of a parliamentary *coup* that can instal a new government without a direct appeal to the electorate. Provided we can secure a number of safeguards to defend the interests of the electorate, I would support proportional representation. We need to aim to win a majority of votes. Otherwise we will not have the authority to remove American nuclear bases or to impose our will on the City of London. Thatcher's authority rests largely on the absence of any real alternative. If she overreaches herself, there will be a

response from below and her authority could disappear overnight. I'm sure that even when we get PR, we will discover
deficiencies in its operation. There simply cannot be a perfect
voting mechanism under a system of indirect democracy.

*What worries me is that unless Labour discusses and agrees on the
best possible form of PR, we might well be lumbered with an
unacceptable version at the end of the decade. The Labour Left
seems unable to grasp that a system which serves a minority Tory
government would not help a socialist Labour government.*

The SDP put down a motion here at the GLC calling for an
investigation into how we could have PR in GLC elections. We
voted it down because it contained dreadful right-wing
phrases about the 'need to combat Labour extremism'. The
Labour Right and the Tory 'wets' voted in its favour. It's that
sort of line-up which worries and alienates the Labour Left
from even considering the question. They see the natural
allies of the Social Democrats as the only supporters for PR.

*That doesn't strike me as a very strong counter-argument. One
could argue that the 'natural supporters' of the present iniquitous
'winner-takes-all' system are Margaret Thatcher, Norman Tebbit
and the bulk of the Conservative Party. I think that the arguments
for establishing a Labour Party Commission on Electoral Reform
are overwhelming in order to ensure that any new system is more
democratic in terms of representation. I know that all this seems
abstract with a 144-seat Tory majority, but many things can
happen over the next five years.*

I do not dispute that a system of PR has its attractions. For
instance, it would remove the problem that many Labour
people vote for the Alliance in the South-East not because
they have switched parties, but in order to get the Tory out.
Under PR the votes of Labour supporters in the Tory shires
would not be wasted. We are being told that this is Labour's
lowest share of the popular vote since 1918. It certainly seems

that way, but I am convinced that under a different electoral system our vote would not have fallen to the same extent, since the Southern Labour voter would have known that his or her vote could return a Labour MP in the final topping-up process. A variation of the German system, which allows everyone to vote positively, is perhaps the biggest justification for PR.

A Socialist Economic Policy

You have just said that the economic strategy defended by the Labour leadership during this election was utterly unconvincing. In a number of articles in Labour Herald *and several speeches you have argued that the Alternative Economic Strategy devised by Labour in 1973–74 and developed after 1979 is no longer sufficient to meet the scale of the economic disaster. What would you see as the major planks of a credible socialist economic policy which could be implemented by a Left government in this country?*

I think we could see a Left government before this decade is over, and it is therefore a realistic question. The first argument we have to get across is that we need to control the flow of capital. This means curbing the speculators in the City of London. Providing you use the terminology of people's everyday experiences and not some turgid economic jargon, you can win back the lost voters. It shouldn't be difficult to explain to working people that a Labour government intends to use the billion pounds a month that currently leave the country to rebuild the economy and the welfare state. Every audience I have addressed has responded overwhelmingly in favour of such a suggestion. Ironically even the Institute of Bankers was not unfavourable to the idea when I spoke there recently. Informally many of them told me after my talk: 'Well, we know this is nonsense which can't go on indefinitely. We're simply making as much money while we can.' I think we could reduce the question of the control of capital and the control of the banks and finance houses to a very few simple and effective slogans, for which we could campaign and win support.

What would be much more difficult, though equally important, would be to argue for an extension of public ownership into the profitable sectors of the economy. By the end of this decade the 'information sector' will in all probability be providing jobs for half the total workforce in the country. That is why Thatcher has to try and destroy British Telecom, which is the most successful state enterprise in the country today. It is at the heart of that area of the British economy which is going to grow in the coming years. Thatcher has to move towards privatization in order to carry through the shift of power in the economy to which she is so ruthlessly committed. For Labour it is essential to renationalize British Telecom if the Tories succeed in privatization, but not simply to stop there.

It will be necessary to create state monopolies based on workers' control and workers' self-management, and to move qualitatively away from the dreadful existing examples, totally unresponsive to consumers, which are responsible for the hostility to public enterprise that undoubtedly exists. Now, everyone will say the opinion polls show that nobody wants nationalization, but we can't as a political party abdicate our responsibility and rely on opinion polls to guide us through the next general election. We've got to go out and convince people. Over the last fifteen years only one Labour politician has argued seriously in favour of public ownership: Tony Benn. But one person can't do it on his or her own. It requires the bulk of the leadership, a large chunk of the PLP, the unions and the activists to move together. Then we could see shifts of opinion on many issues. The whole of the party leadership needs to be driven out of parliament, if necessary with cattle prods since they find it a very attractive place, and forced to stomp up and down the country talking to ordinary people and trying to convince them. This is their real job. You can't win the ideological battle for these policies in the space of an election campaign.

Thatcher won in 1979 partly because, for four whole years, she had conducted a national teach-in with the help of key sectors of the Establishment. We now need to do something similar. All our efforts, on every level, have to be focused on winning the ideological and emotional commitment that is needed if we are ever to implement socialist policies. A weakness during this campaign was the inability of our leaders, even those who agreed with conference decisions, to translate the wordy resolutions into practical policies and pithy catchwords that could appeal to the mass of working people. The details of implementing our policies have clearly not been worked out. When we took over the GLC, we had already discussed a lengthy blueprint of what was needed and what we were going to do. This enabled many of the new left-wing councillors to have the commitment to implement policies and the confidence to argue for them, in the face of near-universal hostility.

The Labour Party needs to do this for itself on a national scale. I don't think I've ever seen anything as depressing as the last election campaign, when so many Labour leaders, in the middle of arguments with the Tories, suddenly realized that their policies didn't add up and crumbled in front of the TV cameras. It was embarrassing. They didn't have the confidence to win the debate because they didn't believe in their own policies. Our position on Polaris fell to bits because no sod had actually gone away and worked out the concrete mechanism of how this was to be done, what (if anything) was to be put in its place, and so on. Confusion reigned supreme. You could see committed unilateralists of the left suddenly find themselves arguing for more spending on defence. Others discovered that they simply couldn't answer all the questions on the doorstep. This was a terrible indictment of the Party. We must never go into another election campaign in the same state.

Before we move off the economy I would like to ask a related question. Surely any figure left-Labour government that seeks to implement the sort of radical economic programme you have outlined will come under very heavy fire from international capitalism. It seems to me that a vital component of such a programme must be the closest possible links with the labour movements throughout Western Europe. This is where the traditional anti-EEC campaign has no answers whatsoever. It was hardly mentioned in this election, presumably because the omnipotent opinion polls said it was not an election issue. I am in favour of breaking with any constraints imposed on British socialism by European capital. But to ignore the positive side of Europeanism – the potential of a powerful working-class unity – seems to be both self-defeating and an encouragement to that deep-rooted jingoism within certain working-class sectors to which you have already referred. This blankness on Europe is especially noticeable on the Labour Left, which is otherwise developing some positive positions on the level of foreign policy.

I find it a bit depressing that we do limit our attitude to Europe to just being anti-Common Market. If there were any real prospect of European unity, with a single European Parliament and Pan-European Conservative and Socialist Parties, I would accept and welcome the prospect without hesitation. If this came about, it would create the potential for a complete transformation of the world economy. It would be worth fighting for such an objective. That we seem to have totally lost sight of such a possibility is tragic. If there is a further economic deterioration over the next few years and we experience a massive slump in the capitalist economy, I think that both Kohl and Thatcher will be out of office. In such a context the only way a left-Labour government in

Britain could survive would be by working with other left governments in Europe and the Third World. There is an enormous potential in Europe. A socialist Common Market could aid in transforming the cycles of poverty that dominate the Third World, by developing a non-exploitative relationship and bypassing the two power blocs. I'd accept a United Europe tomorrow, but that is a bit different from the present EEC, which appears to me to be like a giant version of the GLC bureaucracy. It is a mechanism purely for the free movement of capital, and that is something which is not in the interests of working people. The biggest defect of the EEC bureaucracy is that it generates anti-Europeanism, and not just in Britain. We have a lot to learn from the workers movement in Greece, Italy and the rest of Europe.

The Labour Leadership

I agree with you, but everything you've said so far is premised on a Labour leadership which doesn't exist. I think it is fair to say that the choice we are being offered for the leadership, the 'dream-ticket' of Fleet Street, is not likely to dispel the gloom that has descended on the activist core of the Labour movement since the defeat of 9 June 1983. The choice is especially depressing in the light of the very substantial reforms that have been won inside the Party and which have helped to transform the Constituency Labour Parties (CLPs). Also the Labour GLC has shown that it is possible to fight back and even begin to win people to ideas that are anathematized by the media and the leadership of all political parties in parliament. What would you say to CLP activists in the present situation? Who should they vote for in the forthcoming elections for the Leadership and Deputy Leadership of the Labour Party?

I would say that we have been terribly unlucky. Benn's defeat in Bristol East was a real blow. Otherwise I think there would have been a very good chance of Benn winning. It wouldn't have been a foregone conclusion, but I think Kinnock would have been squeezed out and Benn would have won on the final ballot. What this shows, I suppose, is how right Benn has been over the last few years constantly to say that we cannot build it all up around leading people. We've always taken that as a warning against possible betrayals, of which there is a long record in our movement. But I think it also meant that leaders could be killed, die a natural death or lose an election. There is now the huge problem of a major generation gap inside the PLP between Benn and a whole range of people who are now in their thirties, but lack experience or the stature necessary to lead the Party at the moment. When Benn gets back at the next election or by-election, he will still be the obvious candidate of the Left for some time to come. In the meantime we should follow Benn's advice over the years to build structures which prevent reliance on any individual, but that is a long-term task.

To get back to your question. I suppose at the end of the day, after much thought and agonizing, and after the maximum pressure to squeeze commitments out of him, people will, with the greatest reluctance, vote for Kinnock against Hattersley in the final round. Many of us will vote for Heffer in the first round, but the way the union votes have been lined up the result seems to be a foregone conclusion. I must say that our support should not be unconditional. We must try and get a minimum pledge from Kinnock that (a) there will be no further expulsions from the party; (b) there will be no re-opening of the question of mandatory re-selection as some of the 'soft lefts' in parliament are proposing; and (c) no retreat will be made on the principle of the electoral college to elect the two party leaders. If Kinnock is not prepared to give these assurances, I don't think we should vote for him. There would then be no real difference between him and the other half of the 'dream', Roy

Hattersley. I don't think the Left should incur the odium of being responsible for installing another Harold Wilson as party leader.

I hope that under the pressure of Heffer's candidature and the CLPs, Kinnock will give us assurances on these questions. It would indeed be ironic if he didn't, but Hattersley did. It may be improbable, but if that happens we might have to vote accordingly. These three questions are crucial for the Party. On policy questions there have to be and must be more discussion, debate and even changes. That is natural. But on purges and party democracy we should not give an inch. I know that there are people like the Labour Co-ordinating Committee who believe that the purge will stop with *Militant*, but it really will not and no concessions are permissible on this front. Everyone in the Party hierarchy is aware that *Militant* is not a real threat to the Right. It is the independent Left in the CLPs which is perceived as a cancer that needs to be stopped. Sometimes I think that John Golding's[2] NEC will decree that the GLC members are ineligible for membership because we meet separately as a group.

Ireland

One of the media's hate campaigns against you has centred on your attitude to the British presence in Ireland. There was a concocted uproar when you invited Gerry Adams to visit you in London and the Tories utilized the Prevention of Terrorism Act to prevent him entering the country. This was also one of the arguments utilized by the Labour Right to deprive the Brent East CLP from nominating you as their parliamentary candidate. How do you feel about the fact, one of history's real ironies, that Gerry Adams is

---

2. John Golding was then chairman of the organizational sub-committee of the Labour Party's National Executive Committee and, in that capacity, ringleader of the witch-hunt against Militant Tendency and other Labour Party Marxists.

now a member of the House of Commons, while you are still ensconced at the GLC?

I spent so long trying to get into the House of Commons. Now Gerry Adams gets in and doesn't want to take his seat. Life just isn't fair! More seriously, I think that Ireland, which we haven't touched on until now, is an extremely relevant question. It reveals a terrible weakness in Labour's political and programmatic armoury. We haven't discussed Labour's defence policies as yet, but the obvious weakness here is getting rid of nuclear weapons while remaining in NATO. This is an absurdity. We should take a leaf out of the book of Swedish and Austrian social-democracy on this one. Our policy on Ireland, on the other hand, would paralyse a Labour Government from the very start. Unless the Party changes its attitude on Ireland, a new Labour Government would find itself using the apparatus of repression in Ireland from its first day in office. Wilson and Callaghan had a compliant Labour Party and could get away with that, but there is no way the present Labour Party and the new PLP would accept five years in which a Labour Secretary of State for Northern Ireland was responsible for internment, trial without jury, deaths of children via plastic bullets and all the horrendous things which previous Labour governments have done. Such things done to black people in a more distant colony would cause uproar.

Therefore Ireland is a time-bomb for Labour unless we change course. You can get through an election without having a decent policy on Ireland, but it will erupt in the most terrible split within the Party if we win. I wouldn't have thought a Labour government could stay in Ireland for more than two years. It's the absolute maximum. We have to go into an election pledged to withdrawal within two years. That's the maximum time you can allow for a transition based on a negotiated disengagement. It's the time you would need to organize the finances necessary to maintain the welfare state provisions in the North, which the South couldn't fund at this stage. We must face up to this problem. Otherwise you would have a permanent war within the PLP. Because every time someone was killed by a plastic bullet or worse, you would have an uproar in the PLP.

There is, of course, another aspect of this question which we all tend to ignore because it is never talked about in the media. In every colonial war the army of the metropolitan power involved has invariably become more corrupted by the experience. Extremely sinister currents have emerged within the officer corps of the Army itself. This is characterized by a hostility to all politicians, a distaste and impatience of democratic procedures and norms, etc. This can sometimes have extremely negative consequences in the metropolitan country itself. Spain, Portugal and France offer many instructive lessons in this regard.

Our Army and police have undoubtedly been 'politicized': the Army in Northern Ireland, and the police by the role successive governments have expected them to play in maintaining order in areas that are suffering from the economic policies of the government. With the return of the Tories all these pressures are going to build up. Inevitably the police will be pushed towards more use of arms, more modernized riot-control, more public surveillance. The less you spend on social welfare the more you spend on the police.

The Present State of the Left

Let us briefly return to the state of the Left in the Labour Party. During the Deputy Leadership campaign (an event which Foot and Kinnock blame for the election defeat), we came fairly close to victory. That campaign now appears as the high point of the Left in recent years. There was a time when it seemed that journals such as London Labour Briefing, which is both creative and non-

secturian, could act as an umbrella to unite the disparate lefts inside the CLPs. At the moment, however, the picture is one of disarray. The choice seems to be either to work with some 'well-defined grouping (to put it euphemistically) organized around Militant, Socialist Organiser *or* Socialist Action, *or to be confined to one's CLP. The problem with these groups is that they do not and cannot organize the Left as a whole. Where does that leave individual socialists in the Labour Party, especially in the face of an assault by the Right and the prospects of a 'dream-ticket' in power inside the Party?*

I think there is a persistent problem in the organized British Left, which also exists in other advanced capitalist countries. We have a large number of small groups of activists, who shift backwards and forwards from split to fusion to split. I find it incredible just how much of the present generation of the British Left, in an age range of 35–55, have been in the same things together and expelled each other on numerous occasions. Many of the antagonisms built up twenty years ago are still colouring debates inside the Labour Party on the way forward. This is extremely damaging for the Left as a whole.

What do we do about it? It's not easy. It's always been possible to unite the Left for common goals such as taking over the GLC, Benn's campaign for the Deputy Leadership, democratic reforms of the Party constitution, etc. Once the Left experiences defeat it turns on itself, becomes intro-verted and looks for betrayals within its own ranks. Granted that all of us make an endless number of mistakes and errors, the structure of the Left is such that before you've really had time to think through that you've made a mistake, admit it to yourself and then to others, you've been denounced in the most bitter fashion. This normally has the effect of causing the individual concerned to move away from the Left, first organizationally and then politically. I think that the Left needs to be much more supportive. You've got to be fairly certain that someone has gone over to the politics of pure careerism before you start kicking them around the room. I suppose it is understandable, given the almost permanent record of betrayal by Labour leader after Labour leader, that people spend a lot of time waiting for the next one to go over. There are many cases, however, of people whom we've lost who might have been retained if we'd engaged in comradely debate rather than uncomradely denunciations. If your main function is building your own membership, it is inevitable that you end up with interminable attacks on other left groupings. The amount of time left activists spend rolling around in hysterics, reading the attacks made by one grouping against another, has always amazed me. Unless this method of organization is altered, it will be difficult to unite the Left.

The Trade-Union Bloc Vote

One feature of the election results of June 1983, as of April 1979, has been the desertion of a significant proportion of skilled workers to the Tories. It may be temporary, but it is a fact of political life. Now many of these skilled workers, through their trade-union membership, are, formally speaking, affiliated members of the Labour Party. Here we have a situation which does not exist anywhere else in the world, or even in any other political party in Britain. You can be a member of the Labour Party, but when you go to vote in local or national elections you can vote against your own party. What this indicates is that the trade-union bloc vote that dominates Party conferences is not very representative. The Tebbit proposals,[3] if implemented, could lead to a catastrophic

3. Employment Minister Norman Tebbit's 1982 Green Paper on trade-union reform proposed that the present automatic political levy within the trade union affiliated to the Labour Party (from which individual members may 'contract out')

decline in formal Labour membership. Don't you think that the problem needs to be tackled rapidly by the Party itself?

The matter is beginning to be discussed, and a number of trade-union leaders and people like Eric Heffer and Michael Meacher are coming up with proposals to modify the situation. There is also a legal angle. As long as millions of trade unionists remain affiliated members they cannot be deprived of their right to vote, no matter how it is done. I have no doubt that if we changed the voting system at Conference, some trade-union leaders might well resort to the courts. It is true that you can occasionally get a better judgement from a court than from any committee run by John Golding, but in my opinion internal disputes must be settled within the movement. We should not bring the judicial arm of the state into the Labour movement.

The point I was making was a different one. It is perfectly possible for Swedish Social Democrats and Austrian Socialists to have mass membership parties without the mediation of a 'bloc vote'. In both cases the trade unions help to finance these parties. In Britain we have a situation where the Conservative Party has a much higher individual membership than Labour. We seem to have the worst of both worlds: a membership level that cannot be compared to Sweden's or Austria's and a bloc vote which is clearly only partially representative of the rank-and-file. This can only institutionalize a depoliticization of Labour, confining it to purely electoral activities.

I agree that affiliated membership has become a formality. It's because it's such a cheap thing to do. The weekly subscription is so insignificant that most trade unionists can't be bothered to 'contract out' of Labour Party membership.

---

should be outlawed and replaced by a system of 'contracting in' to the Labour Party. Tebbit himself has since become secretary for trade and industry, but his name is still associated with the attack on Labour–trade-union links.

Hence you can construct this huge paper membership that enables people to cast bloc votes here, there and everywhere. I think it would be more realistic to equalize the subscription paid by trade unionists and an individual member of a CLP. Even if we reduced the rate slightly, it would bring in more money and mean more to the trade unionist in question. The alternative, which I'm increasingly beginning to favour, is a major shift of emphasis to workplace branches. The key to carrying out our programme after we've won an election is having mass support. I do not believe you can get mass support based on a CLP structure. That old SWP gibe about a 'resolution machine' and 'resolutionary politics' is true. People turn up once a month to a completely artificial structure, which exists only because the Boundary Commissioners have decreed that these are the parameters of the new constituency. They don't respect communities or anything else. The only thing that holds a CLP together is the desire to win the next election or the struggle to control this or that part of the local machine so that they can get their councillors elected. This is necessary, but clearly insufficient for a party committed to change.

If we were to shift the emphasis and draw the trade unions into the activity of building workplace branches, then all those areas from which the Labour Party is currently excluded because the National Union of Teachers (NUT) or the National Association of Local Governement Officers (NALGO) aren't affiliated to the Labour Party, could be organized directly by the Labour Party. Even where there is affiliation, it would help to encourage a regular political debate in the workplace, in the shop, factory or school. That's where we're going to win. This will also bring the experience of working people to bear upon the determination of our programme and policies, in a much more effective way than through relying on opinion polls or media pundits. For instance, on the question of nationalizing the top 25 companies, it would be much better if we had direct communication with the workers of these 25 companies and discussed with them how it would operate in their workplace. Until this debate is shifted from someone's front room to the point of production or distribution, it won't get fleshed out. This is the method I would prefer to sort out the bloc-vote problem, rather than getting involved in interminable wrangles with the unions. We should shift the party away from a pure CLP structure to workplace structures, now that workplace branches can affiliate directly to the General Management Committees of local parties. Such a structure would also benefit the workers. If, for instance, there was a problem of closure or redundancies, you would have a ready-made political structure which workers could use to involve the local CLP, Labour councillors and the nearest MP. I think you'll find that the Swedish party has a much greater workplace involvement than we have. This is the way we have to go. Otherwise we spend all our time in CLP structures – which I know you've had to fight to attend – but the rest of us are often quite happy to have another meeting to attend so we can give the CLP a miss.

Women's Liberation

Of all the movements that grew up in the sixties, the one that offered a clear glimpse of a future which was totally different from the present and the past was the women's liberation movement. Feminism has had a profound impact on a large minority of the population in North America and even in Western Europe. What do you think has been feminism's impact in the political arena? You are one of the few leaders of the Labour Movement clearly identified with a strong commitment to feminism and sexual liberation. Could you explain how this came about?

I suppose because my actual involvement in politics coincided with the birth and growth of the women's liberation movement. There was clearly a cross-fertilization of ideas, and I was on the fringes of quite a few of their meetings. I have always felt that the Labour Party's almost exclusive concentration on the employed male white working class was a weakness. My own view is that you can't transform society solely on that basis. You need a coalition which includes skilled and unskilled workers, unemployed, women and black people, as well as the sexually oppressed minorities. A socialist political party must act broadly for and with all the oppressed in our society. This means that *we* have to change. I'm opposed to cynical attempts to co-opt the women's movement just because we can get votes out of it. The Labour Party must listen to what the women are saying and then change itself.

What makes me particularly interested is my own background outside politics, which, as I've already indicated, involved the study of natural history. This drives some of my friends mad, but it simply is the case that I have come to left-wing politics not through a theoretical Marxist background, but via a study of animal behaviour and evolution. The present domination/subordination relationships between the sexes date back 50,000 years, when humankind was at an extremely primitive stage of cultural development. Yet this primitive aspect lingers on and women remain oppressed. We have moved on since then: there has been a growth of language, art and culture, culminating in the growth of modern technology. All this means that the prerequisites for the liberation of women are present today. The fact that women have every right to share power and to control their own bodies is something that must be accepted. Men have to surrender their position of power over women – a role which has its origin in that initial change in the pattern of food acquisition and hunting.

It won't happen easily though, will it? Some men on the left assume that with the abolition of capitalism everything will flow smoothly.

No, of course not. You can abolish capitalism and still see a continuation of gender subordination. I happen to believe that you can move away from institutionalized male domination and actually remain within capitalism. Capitalism has utilized the oppression of women. It didn't create it. You can have a form of liberation within the present system whereby women become mirror images of men: exploitative, aggressive, dominating and subjugating others. The question of capitalism isn't completely tied in with this question. I don't believe that men will be able to achieve socialism while exploiting women. We cripple ourselves by dominating women. The gender roles established centuries ago have led to stereotypes which are passed on from generation to generation. It might sound a bit glib, but isn't too far from the truth to say that it is the woman who values and cherishes and protects life, and that very often it is the man who is prepared to exploit and terminate life to advance his own position. We have to break away from those sexual roles, which are replicated in every aspect of life – in the school, the common room, in the Labour Party and everywhere men and women gather. The old division of labour still dominates as we approach the twenty-first century. What an indictment of our civilization! This is where the intervention of the women's movement has been beneficial. It offers men and women the chance to break out of a relationship that is totally destructive of human potential. We all make wonderful speeches about how the present educational system denies working-class children the right to achieve their full potential. Yet the nature of our relationship to the women we live with denies them the chance to develop their full potential. This is so deeply ingrained that it affects *all* men, including those who guard against it, denounce it in public, and so on. It is crazy that something which began when humankind were primitive hunters should still dominate our advanced industrial societies.

I tend to agree with you, but let us return for a moment to the problems within the Labour Party on this question. It is now clear that a large layer of socialist feminists have joined the Party over the last few years, particularly since the democratic reforms achieved at Wembley. This is partially symbolized by the fact that Lynne Segal and Sheila Rowbotham, two of the authors of Beyond the Fragments, *are now members of the Labour Party and that Hilary Wainwright is employed by the GLC. In some ways the most vigorous struggle against the Right at the 1982 Labour Party Conference was mounted by these socialist feminists. Their arguments were unanswerable, so the bloc vote was used by the Right to hammer them into the ground under the direction of Gwyneth Dunwoody, Betty Boothroyd, et al. Do you think that socialist feminists have a future inside the Labour Party?*

I think they have the major future inside the party. The changes they eventually make within the Labour Party will change the nature of socialism in Britain. I think they will make it more likely we will achieve socialism in Britain. As women change the nature of the Labour Party, it will become much more possible to reach women who have voted Conservative all their life, but who share many of the values of feminism, though obviously not expressed as such. We have to reach those women. There are millions of them who have been denied a collective work experience, which is the traditional Labour Movement way of building its base and recruiting people to a class and developing within that class. The alternative way, which we have to explore, is to reach these women who have not had a collective experience as women via the feminist movement. That means changing the way we operate, which is still so hideously vicious.

All the little gestures that spill over into politics are very revealing. The way we operate, the way we put each other down and turn most women off. I remember speaking to a woman who was a prospective parliamentary candidate in 1979 and asking why she hadn't stood again. She said there was no way she was going to subject herself to being poked, prodded and humiliated, with people trying to trip you up *en route* to a safe seat and then sitting in a back room with all the other competitors trying to undermine each other's self-confidence and upstaging each other. She said that wasn't the way in which we were going to achieve socialism. Too bloody right. That's a hold-over from jousting. It has more in common with that closing frame in *The Godfather* where Michael Corleone, having eliminated all his rivals, receives his aides who come in and bend to kiss his ring, which is a symbol of his power. We behave like that all the time in the Labour Party. The only differences between us and the Mafia is that we've stopped killing each other. If the Labour Party was based in Sicily, no doubt the Right would have some of us rubbed out on the way to meetings. Some of the Left would reciprocate. We are still using those same basic patterns of power and manipulation. It is simply not appropriate for a species which has reached the technological level that we have today. It's actually a recipe for mass suicide.

Part Two

The New Labour Left

Since our last conversation, several months ago, a number of significant changes have taken place in British politics. As I see it, there are four key elements in the present situation that are likely to stay with us in one form or another until the next elections. I exclude the question of the GLC and local democracy, which we will be discussing separately. At the time of our last talk, the 1983 Labour Party conference had not yet taken place and speculation was therefore in order. Now we have a new elected leadership and the 'dream ticket' is in power. The situation needs to be discussed soberly, without demagogy, since two important issues are at stake: winning the next election and preventing a repetition of the Mitterrand and González experiences in France and Spain. Secondly, Tony Benn has fought and won the Chesterfield by-election, with Labour presenting a unified façade. You participated in the Chesterfield campaign, and it would be useful to record your views on it. Thirdly, we are talking in the middle of the miners' strike – the first major industrial upheaval to confront this Tory government, which has responded with a massive display of police power. Lastly, one gets the feeling that for the first time since 1979 or, more specifically, since the Falklands episode, Thatcher's own position within the Conservative Party is much weaker than before (not least because of the local democracy question), and a number of scandals involving corruption in her family have erupted.

That's one question . . . ?

The Mood inside the Party

Take it as four, if you like. Let's start with the situation inside the Labour Party. My own feeling from numerous discussions with rank-and-file CLP activists – and I am referring now to those who don't belong to any of the far-left currents – is that while none of them is particularly sanguine or happy with the present leadership and few trust it to deliver the goods, they are nonetheless obsessed with winning the next election, understandably so, and do not want to do anything that could damage that possibility. It is almost as if a sub-conscious collective decision has been taken to defer debate until after the general elections. What is your assessment of the mood inside the party?

I think that is the perspective of CLP activists. That's what I pick up, travelling round the country. People have recovered from the shock of June 1983, but one must remember that it was a very, very traumatic shock. We saw the Labour Party come close to being pushed into third place. When Neil Kinnock was elected party leader, there was no certainty that the decline could be halted and people were therefore extremely worried and suspicious. Since that time Kinnock has succeeded in reversing the trend and we are now neck-and-neck with the Tories in the polls. The SDP is in an utterly demoralized state, and many of its friends in Fleet Street are beginning to desert the sinking ship. Some polls are even showing us slightly ahead. There is thus a great sigh of relief inside the Party. From the brink of destruction, we have moved back to a position where it is possible to conceive of a Labour victory at the next elections. I don't think anyone should underestimate just how many people in the Party really did believe that we are facing the prospect of being completely smashed. I, personally, did not think that it was

ever really on, but many people did. So now there is a
tremendous desire to avoid anything that might damage the
Party and put the Tories back in office for a third term. Even
the most ultra-left purist must be able to see what a disaster
this would represent for the British working class.

There is another factor in operation. The memory of the
disasters inflicted by the last Labour governments has
receded with the passage of time and the experience of
Thatcher's regime. By the time of the next election there will
be a whole generation of people in much the same position as
I was in 1964: they will have no memory of a Labour Government, they will expect a lot and will be extremely enthu-
siastic. With reference to another segment of your question, I
think I would draw a distinction between what has happened
here in terms of the Labour Left over the past thirty years,
and the Mitterrand and González governments. In France
and particularly in Spain there had been a long period of
right-wing government. Not only had memories faded, but
there were few politicians around, with the exception of
Mitterrand himself, who had served in a government of the
Left. You would have to be in your seventies to have played
any role in the movement in Spain at the time of the Civil
War. This highlights a fact which could prove to be of crucial
importance. For although, as I said just now, a large section
of people will see the next Labour government as something
completely new, there is still quite a sizeable layer that has a
historical memory, that remembers how the Wilson and
Callaghan governments failed over the last twenty years.
This knowledge will prevent many CLP activists from simply
sitting around (except at standing-ovation time), trusting the
leadership and then observing the collapse of a Labour
government under pressure. I don't think we'll have either to
relive the Mitterrand/González experience or repeat the
disasters of 1964–70 and 1974–79 all over again. A third
failure for a Labour government could well prove fatal,

because it would strengthen every fascist reflex in British society. It would be dangerous to imagine that a third failure would automatically create space for the socialist Left. We are in a different period today. Don't forget that the abysmal failure of Callaghan coincided with an upsurge of the National Front, which Thatcher partially confiscated with all her talk of combating 'alien cultures' in our midst. France and Spain are experiencing what we did in 1964–66: A new generation of activists are learning their lessons the hard way. It is when you go through a long period without a left government that there is a very real danger of complacency. Some of the things that were said by the Left about the 1945 government were really naive, but, in a sense, they were finding their way as there hadn't been a majority Labour government before.

The New Leader

What do you think about the Kinnock style: the image politics, the American-style TV commercials, which no Labour leader in the past ever used in the same way? Attlee was never tempted to combat the Churchill cult by promoting his own. Wilson pushed a certain idea, based on his notion of modernization. The impression one gets with Kinnock (and this has even been remarked upon by the TV critic of The Observer*) is that he is so careful not to put a foot wrong* vis-à-vis *the media (in other words, the consensual Establishment that dominates British politics) that he comes over as a politician with a lot of froth, but little substance. This packaging by the PR-conscious advisers around him may or may not help his image, but in terms of rebuilding Labour as a campaigning party it seems to be an utter disaster.*

Actually, I don't think it is right to say that Kinnock is being packaged by a group of professionals. The people around him wish they had that influence on him, but I can detect individual concerns and moans that Kinnock sails off in the direction he wants to go, leaving all that little coterie around him wondering what he will commit them to next. I think we are dealing here with his own gut instinct about how to establish himself in the popular mind. I am not at all certain that people like Charles Clarke and Patricia Hewitt[1] were really running him in the way that some people suspected. If they had been, I doubt that Kinnock's style would be anything like what you see today. People wake up and open the papers to find they're committed to something, as I've often done in terms of an initiative around Ireland. He's doing it in a different way. He isn't just sitting down, taking the broad consensus around him and then trundling on. He's very much striking out on his own.

You can't understand the difference between Kinnock and Wilson unless you look at their backgrounds. Wilson went through the position of being a key civil servant during the war, completely involved in controls and planning, then served throughout the length of the first Labour government, and then spent thirteen years in opposition, occupying an often pivotal position in the struggles between left and right. Thus Wilson became prime minister after twenty years in, or close to, the centres of power. Neil Kinnock, on the other hand, went from a very stable, secure family background in a small town in Wales, where there is still a strong sense of community, through grammar school and university and then, with a three-year gap in lecturing, straight into Parliament. He has never held any office whatsoever, and so he will clearly take quite a time to establish the self-confidence that he can run the governmental machine. It was easier for Wilson to put on this convincing managerial show, because he had convinced himself that he could manage it.

---

1 Charles Clarke: personal assistant to Neil Kinnock. Patricia Hewitt: former general-secretary of the National Council for Civil Liberties and currently Neil Kinnock's press officer.

Kinnock hasn't yet had to tackle all those key civil servants who operate so effectively around the prime minister.

That may be true. But the choice he has made – the one traditional to all Labour leaders and accepted by the British establishment – is to lead the party from the centre or the right of centre. It is this that is very worrying for the future. It's not a question of his particular personality.

I think personality matters, because it is the area that will pose major problems for the building of a structure around the party leadership to counter-balance the power and style of the civil service. Most people don't become prime minister without a fairly long period in contact with the civil service; they know what they are going to get into at that stage. But you are right that Neil is leading from the centre, particularly in the positions he has struck on compliance with the law, which are ones I personally wouldn't have chosen to make. However, if you look at some of the positions he has taken on the miners and the NGA dispute, it seems likely that a Wilson or a Callaghan would have condemned the strikes quite shamelessly. There is at least a certain improvement here in comparison with what previous Labour leaders would have said. Kinnock is not as much under the control of part of the establishment as his predecessors were.

In my view, the real struggle is over the nature of the economic problems which the next Labour government will face, the balance of forces within the PLP, and how quickly the Trade Union leaderships will push him to deliver something. Kinnock's decision to establish himself in the popular mind as a nice guy before he starts talking about politics, or to take the stand he has on compliance with the law, does not mean that all that happened in 1964–70 will automatically follow. If Neil Kinnock becomes Prime Minister, he will take over at a point where there has been a revulsion against the Tory government. The mere election of a Labour government will start to bring confidence back to the workers. Those who are prepared to put up with the situation under this present government will immediately feel we can push harder this time. You see it on every local council. Where you have a Tory administration, NALGO and the staff association make a few rumblings but do nothing; as soon as a Labour administration comes in, they're pushing all the time, and you can't help resenting it. Why don't they attack the Tories as hard as they push on us? But that's an inevitable situation. Workers will feel more secure to press forwards as soon as they get that Labour government, and there will be such a backlog that they will be pushing on a whole series of fronts, not just on pay.

The Parliamentary Party

On the question of balance within the PLP, I'm certain that, whether or not the vote on selection is open to all party members, the constituencies will still be overwhelmingly of the left. Nor do I think that the balance in the trade unions will dramatically tip one way or the other. Those two areas of pressure will still be there. The really dramatic change will be in the PLP. We've now got 209 MPs. It may be assumed that no more than half-a-dozen will be de-selected – although even that may be an optimistic figure, given that it was smaller last time and that a lot of the dross has gone or been driven out. A further ten, twenty or perhaps thirty of the present 209 will retire by then. So, if Labour wins the 326 seats necessary to gain an absolute majority at the next election, the fact is that almost half of the PLP will then be new, and probably over more than half. They will nearly all come from the seats we win off the Tories – which are by definition the most active parliamentary seats, where you usually have a hard-left or soft-left majority that will overwhelmingly choose people who have not been MPs before. With this new influx of people, all with fairly radical instincts, the situation will be like in 1945. But this time the PLP will already contain, not just Tony Benn but many other people who have been through the failures of the last twenty years. I believe this new combination will be a much more potent force, combining the old left in Parliament with a mass of new MPs who will want the Labour government to deliver.

There will also be huge economic pressures on it: unemployment will be well in excess of what it is now; there will have been a further contraction of public services; and every section of British society will be starting to demand change. A third factor, though much less tangible, is also present. When I go all round the country, I really do detect a mood of confidence starting to build up – not in the sense that people think we can win, take over or transform society, but a confidence that comes from saying, we're not giving any more. It can't be found everywhere. But it's there in certain key industries, some towns and cities, and so on. You just feel that there's a gathering tide of demands for reform.

It may all be statistical luck, but it is almost as if there were a political cycle of change. In 1906 the Tories were electorally demolished by the Liberal landslide and the foundations of the welfare state were laid. Four decades followed, punctuated by unemployment, defeated strikes, a defection from the Labour Party, Tory appeasement of Mussolini and Hitler, the Second World War and then a reforming Labour Government. Those were the last real reforms achieved by any government. In the four decades since Attlee we have seen consensus politics based on Keynesian principles, and two Labour Governments which were incapable of any major reforms and unable to resist either the International Monetary Fund or the City of London. (A large section of the members of the Wilson and Callaghan Cabinets have since defected to their natural habitat.) This was followed by Thatcher, attempting to implement the Selsdon Programme of the last Heath Government. She succeeded to a large extent because the working-class movement, especially in England, had been very badly demoralized by its experience of Labour in office.

I have a real sense that there is a change of mood taking place. It is happening slowly and unevenly, but its net result will be a Tory electoral defeat. It is now so long since the last great reforms that a new Labour administration would be under very heavy pressure from the trade unions, CLPs, CND. It would be wrong to rule out in advance that Kinnock will have a sympathetic response to these pressures. I think he is different from Wilson/Callaghan; but more importantly, he will be operating in a changed context as far as the PLP is concerned. The potential for a fundamental and radical change is beginning to develop: there is everything to fight for. Of course, it could all fall to bits, for reasons of which you and I are aware. But it could also turn out to be one of the more radical parliaments, and Labour MPs should ensure that it is if they want to be returned again.

Internal Struggle and the Fight for Marginals

When we spoke at the Labour Briefing *fringe meeting during the London Labour Party conference, you advised party activists not to get sidetracked by internal wranglings, but to employ their energies in ensuring victory in marginal seats. Would you care to enlarge on that, since I noticed some discontent in the audience at that point?*

Certainly! The whole key to our success with the GLC, in terms of how the Left won control, is related to the emphasis we placed on the marginals. Of course we started in areas where there was a chance of de-selecting, and we went ahead and did it with CLP support. But soon we realized that in the end we wouldn't get more than a handful of socialist GLC councillors. We finally got three! You have to understand that there is a basic loyalty-mechanism in the Labour Party which precludes large-scale de-selections. CLPs with a healthy voting record are prepared to tolerate the most appallingly right-wing MPs, provided that he/she visits the constituency regularly, does the case-work, listens to the party, doesn't patronize local activists, and treats opponents with respect. It is when you get a Reg Prentice² that de-selection becomes a real possibility. Arrogance and contempt are intolerable to most members of a General Committee. Also, of course, if the MP is an absolutely bone-idle deadbeat . . .

Or is preparing to defect to the SDP or the Tories?

That makes it easy. In the last GLC election we concentrated on marginal seats held by the Tories and got good, solid candidates into position. That is how I believe we will achieve a major shift in the political composition of the PLP. There is nothing clandestine or conspiratorial about this operation. We are open in our aims. We want more socialists in the PLP!

If you look around at the situation in Britain, there seem to be only mumblings about de-selecting half-a-dozen sitting MPs. I can just see the party spending vast amounts of its time in campaigns to make sure of Deptford's right to re-select, taking months and months of the time of left activists, and then we will find that two or three dozen useless individuals have been selected for seats that we are going to win off the Tories. I don't wish to be misunderstood. I'm not saying that parties which can de-select their MP shouldn't do so; what I'm saying is that the broad role of the left within the party is to focus on the 120 or possibly 140 seats that we must win from the Tories. That is where a dramatic transformation of the PLP will come from. I believe that many activists are still

---

2. Former Labour MP for the Newham North-East constituency, who defected to the Tories after a local campaign was mounted to replace him as the Party's parliamentary candidate for the next elections.

repeating the mistakes of the period after the Benn campaign
for the deputy leadership. A vast amount of effort went in the
first year into trying to get Kinnock and Lestor off the NEC. I
have my doubts whether that was ever worthwhile, especially
in the case of Joan Lestor. After all, she had resigned as a
junior minister in the last Labour government over the question of cuts in education, and the left slate for the NEC
included Margaret Beckett, who had taken her place as
minister. It wasn't the best use of so much of our time in
1982. And then in 1983 we had this herculean struggle to get
hold of the CLPD AGM and to ensure that it did not register as
an approved body, although no one on the Labour right gave
a sod whether the CLPD registered with Walworth Poad or
not. All that time the Left was drawing closer to its most
stunning election defeat of all time – a blow to morale from
which we have not yet recovered. And so, I was absolutely
horrified to hear someone say the other day that the real
struggle was to get Meacher and Blunkett off the NEC,
because they didn't vote correctly on . . . I don't even know
what the bloody issue was. But everybody around was going:
'Oh, no, you've got be be kidding.' It is a real danger on the
British Left, and not just in the Labour Party, that because it
can be such fun abusing each other, we devote a vast amount
of time to this sport. No one on the other side of the class
divide would waste so much time on whether the Duke of
Norfolk should be removed or punished in some way for
upsetting the government in a House of Lords division. They
prefer to surge on and smash the next trade union they can lay
their hands on. We have to work out which are the really big
prizes, and go for them. There is nobody who is so perfect in
their political record that you can say you support them one
hundred per cent. If a group of people get rid of Meacher and
Blunkett, no doubt the same ones will tomorrow want to get
rid of Benn or myself because of a petty tactical difference.
You cannot be in the Labour Party without making com-

promises, as many people who left to form revolutionary groupings have now recognized. Purity, I'm afraid, is what you lose when you join the Labour Party.

Obviously there is a great deal of utterly useless sectarianism and backbiting on the Left, though I would add that it is not restricted to the Left. The Right tends to conceal it much more, keeping its knives for the clubs and boardrooms. Nor are the women's movements or the ethnic communities devoid of in-fighting, but we can agree that it is time- and energy-consuming and can also be soul-destroying. There are probably more burnt-out and charred socialists outside the organized Left than inside its ranks.

Benn's Return to Parliament

Let's move on to discuss the Chesterfield by-election campaign. Some on the Left, and I am thinking mainly of the Socialist Workers Party, have argued that the campaign signalled Tony Benn's capitulation to the forces of law and order within the Labour Party. They have cited and published photographs of Kinnock, Hattersley and Healey on Benn's platform to convince their membership of Benn's betrayal, etc., etc. The fact that yourself, Denis Skinner, Arthur Scargill, Joan Maynard, Eric Heffer and hundreds of other socialists also went up is regarded as unimportant. What was your impression of the campaign? Eric Heffer has made it clear that, in his view, Benn fought a model socialist campaign, and fought it well. How did you feel about it?

If you work inside the Labour Party you have to make tactical compromises, which would not even arise in the purist isolation of a revolutionary grouping outside the Party. This is a hard fact of political life. Labour has Healey and Hattersley within its ranks, and their supporters include a few million inside the working class. It would be dishonest to fight an election on the basis that Labour was a perfect socialist party (even though many of us would like it to become one). Most

Labour voters are aware of this reality. They are also aware that politicians have done many squalid things, but they still vote for them. Even the SWP is aware of this when it calls for a vote for Labour. It does not say: vote for the Labour lefts, but abstain where there are right-wing candidates. In all struggles, including those in the electoral arena, the enemy has to be identified. In this case it is the Tories and the SDP-Liberal Alliance.

Let's look back at the situation which confronted Tony Benn. During that by-election, if he had done *anything* that appeared divisive, he would have provided a field-day for all his opponents. The media would have gone even more beserk than it did, and the result may well have been a major setback for the Left and the working class. I went and heard Benn speaking at meetings and we shared a platform at most of them. His politics were rock-solid. He defended socialism and democracy. I didn't disagree with a single word he said. Chesterfield was not just an election campaign: it was an exercise in mass political education. It should have been videoed and sent to all CLPs as part of a training course in how to conduct electoral struggles. In Chesterfield you had a party which had been represented for twenty years by Eric Varley, a man who should never have been in the Labour Party in the first place, who had done nothing to justify his occupation of that seat on behalf of Labour for two decades, and who then just sloped off to get a well-paid job with Coalite. These were the worst possible circumstances in which to have a by-election – particularly as the press were able to exploit ten years of witch-hunting against Tony Benn in the media.

Benn went into that campaign, fighting with both fists. He personally met with one-third of the constituency and spoke at numerous public and factory-gate meetings, vigorously expounding the political views he has been putting across for years. Talking to people, one had the feeling that for them it had been a political education: a town which for years had been bypassed by all the major currents in the Labour Party suddenly had a concentrated dose of political education, and Benn actually increased the number of people turning out to vote Labour. I cannot imagine a more difficult seat for Tony Benn to have stood in. If it had been an inner-city area in Manchester or Birmingham or London there would have been no problems, but Chesterfield was the kind of seat where a bad Labour campaign and a good Alliance campaign could have put us in real difficulty. Our holding it was a major triumph and certainly one of the things that has started rebuilding confidence. A lot of people are saying that if Tony Benn can go into that sort of seat and win that sort of by-election, then clearly we are on the way back. We are now getting incredible shifts to Labour in by-elections. Opinion polls recently in London showed that if there was a GLC election, Labour would win the biggest majority it has had in London for the last twenty years. In council by-elections in London we are now seeing decisive shifts to Labour. If Benn had lost, it would have demoralized the bulk of CLPs and set back the process of recovery. Instead we are witnessing a process of reconstruction, and a confidence that Thatcher can be defeated on the basis of policies agreed by recent party conferences.

Moreover, the Left has its most effective tribunes back in Parliament, which is not an unimportant fact in the present political situation.

Tony Benn is perfectly well aware that the British media, which are owned or dominated by Tories with a sprinkling of SDP types, is going to dissect everything he says or writes in an attempt to manufacture another row in the pre-election period. So obviously Benn will have to be careful, as Ted Knight and myself have been and will continue to be in this critical period for Labour and the workers movement as a whole. The debates in the party – which, incidentally, are its lifeblood, in contrast to the monolithic charade put on by the Tories for the media every year and dignified by the name 'conference' – must not be had in such a way that we give *The Sun* another front-page cover.

On the other hand, it is worth remembering that the vicious campaign against Tony Benn was sparked off at the time of the Deputy Leadership campaign. The entire media, and not just The Sun, *was attacking Benn. The* Daily Mirror *and* The Guardian *were equally biased and took their lead from off- and on-the-record remarks made by the Shadow Cabinet. It was the deadbeat Peter Shore who described Benn as 'the cuckoo in our nest', and that gave the entire media the green light to savage Benn. They knew that the consensus politicians had decreed a no-holds-barred campaign. Benn was never defended once at that time by the Foot–Kinnock Centre: they passively acquiesced in the slanders and innuendoes. The* Guardian's *reporting of the Deputy-Leadership struggle was a disgrace by any standards. But it was not surprising, given that its Political Editor, Ian Aitken, is an old factotum of Foot – a relationship that stretches from the old* Tribune *via common employment by Lord Beaverbrook down to the present day. It would simply be counter-productive in the medium term to forget these facts.*

I agree, but I think that's the other thing that has changed, however temporarily. It's not just that the Left is exercising a certain self-discipline: it's also that people on the Right who used to devote every weekend speech, in effect, to a denunciation of the Labour Party have desisted from such attacks for some time. An informal cease-fire is being observed by both sides. I believe that this truce, however much it might subjectively depress many activists on the Left, is going to last until the next general election.

Kinnock will have to be a fairly incompetent politician not to get through the next few years without keeping a fairly united party behind him. There is a desperate desire to be united. He can choose the ground on which he attacks the government. Everywhere you go in the party people do actually want Kinnock to succeed. They don't want their worst fears confirmed; they want their best hopes vindicated, and therefore he has everything going for him. Only when a Kinnock government has to start taking decisions about what it does will the ceasefire be transformed either into a struggle for a genuinely radical Labour Party in Parliament or into a long, drawn-out slogging match to defend socialist policies.

The Miners' Strike

If we could come on to the third component of the present situation, we are now seeing an escalation of the miners' strike, with support from the transport workers and the seamen. But what I would like to put to you is the following: the miners' strike in 1984 is very different in character from the 1972–74 strikes which finally toppled the Tory government. This time the miners themselves are disunited, and although they are getting solidarity from other unions, there isn't that spontaneous burst of support that we saw before. Moreover, there was an element of deliberate provocation in MacGregor's decision to close a pit in Yorkshire: he knew perfectly well that it was there that the fuse was shortest. But regardless of whether or not the strike was provoked, we are now in the middle of it, and I'd like to hear your views. Many union activists have told me that, with exceptions such as Eric Heffer and Tony Benn, and probably a few others, the Shadow Cabinet and even the party as a whole have made no attempt to link in with this struggle and push it forward. They do not seem to see that a victory here could have major repercussions for the Tory government and for Labour's own victory.

The mood around the miners' strike is totally different from that in 1974, because these are totally different times. 1972 and 1974 came at the culmination of a 25-year world boom. Workers had developed a lot of confidence and expected full employment and a rising standard of living; then they saw the Heath government challenge a lot of the things they had taken for granted, and they reacted quite firmly and eventually defeated it. The lesson that the Tories drew was that they would have to be much better prepared the next time. They spent the whole of the mid-seventies on a propaganda campaign to convince people that we had to rein in the trade unions and cut back the welfare state – and in this they were echoed by many key people on Labour's front bench. So they won the intellectual ground; they won the hearts and minds of a substantial proportion of the population to the view that these things now had to be done. And from the point of view of the Tory Party they do have to be done, given the change in the nature of the world economy and the problems of British capital. They can't avoid making those sorts of attacks on organized labour. Mrs Thatcher was defeated by the miners in 1980 over the question of pit closures. She admitted it. But now they've planned for it: they've made certain the coal stocks are there; they've opened up the British market to Polish coal imports; they've brought key people into the police force, in the shape of the former boss of the Royal Ulster Constabulary, Sir Kenneth Newman, and others; they've continued the propaganda campaign in the press, which reached a frenzied peak against Arthur Scargill last October; and they've brought in MacGregor, with a track record of getting rid of half the jobs in the steel industry, to do the same job for coal. It is an open provocation. They wish to break the miners because they know that it will demoralize every trade unionist in struggle. If the miners can be broken, anyone can be broken – that's how it will be perceived. And if the miners are broken, there will be a victory celebration by this government. They will crow about it, they will talk about restoring the damage done by the 1980 defeat of Thatcher by the miners. That is why a lot of trade unions, after some reluctance, are now coming in and rallying round. They know that if the miners go down, they will all be substantially damaged. There is a key difference. Capital has prepared for this strike in a way that it hasn't prepared since the General Strike.

The police operation was very well planned. It couldn't have been organized in 24 hours . . .

No. In the same way that during the General Strike the Tories took off the shelf the plans that Labour ministers had drawn up during the minority government in 1924, a lot of the planning which is now being put into operation was most probably started under the last Labour government and accelerated under Thatcher. These plans are now there and ready for use against the workforce, particularly in the sense that the public is being conditioned to accept things it would never have accepted before. Just think what would have happened five years ago if the police had stopped people moving across county boundaries. If, after the last GLC elections, I had made a speech saying that within a few years the police would be stopping people moving across county boundaries, there would have been a whole lot of hysteria about lunatic left-wing nonsense. If, three years ago, we had predicted that the government would try to abolish elections to the GLC, it would all have been dismissed in the same way. They have massively shifted the climate of opinion, but the government's weak point is that it isn't aware of the mood of society as a whole.

I think that the problem for Thatcher and Tebbit and British capital is that they only meet the leadership of the Labour movement. They see the Labour front bench in Parliament, they see Len Murray scuffling around saying, 'Don't break the law, lads!' looking as if he's not long for this world, they see one trade union dispute after another sold out, as the NGA was, as the healthworkers were. And so, they then push forward with these new powers for the police and this attempt to break the miners. When they demand that violence be condemned, they get some equivocating statement rather than a firm denunciation of the government. But although they continue pushing because they detect little resistance at the top, they suddenly run into growing resistance at grassroots level, so that the government could find itself defeated or Thatcher overthrown and replaced by another figure. They are getting all the wrong signals on how to proceed in the miners' dispute, because all the signals come from the top. It's like everything else; if you go back to 1945, all the leading figures in the Labour Party thought that Churchill would be re-elected. Except for Bevan. He had been stomping around the country all the way through the war, and he detected that a tide of change was building up. In one sense, trade union leaders and Labour Party leaders in Parliament are the last people to become aware of the tide that is building up behind them. Therefore, it could take only one slight miscalculation by one police commander to spark off a tremendous public backlash. When people see the police marching up and down the hill, it just doesn't look like Britain. It goes against deeply ingrained mythologies. A lot of middle class people do not want to live in an authoritarian right wing regime; they don't particularly want socialism, or they haven't been persuaded of its benefits for them, but they certainly don't want to live in something which looks like an English-speaking version of Argentina or Chile.

The bourgeois media have made a big issue of a miners' national ballot, on which the miners have previously been very strict. Of course it is all a bit sick. The Guardian didn't ballot its journalists before handing Sarah Tisdall over to the mercy of the Tory judges. And I can see why Scargill, McGahey and the miners' executive decided on this course of action. But on the other hand, if the strike is defeated – which, of course, we all hope it won't be – there will be people in the rank and file of the Union and elsewhere who will say it would have been far better to have had a ballot, because it is far better to be defeated by your own membership than by the state.

Well, I'm not certain that Arthur and the NUM executive decided on this strategy. What probably happened is that there was a strong reaction in key areas like Yorkshire, and I can well understand that Arthur and others don't want to call a ballot at a time when it would split the Union, because there is still a residue of bitterness in South Wales from the time when the rest of the NUM didn't come in. I think this is a great weakness. It's easy to have a ballot over the annual payround or whatever. But it can be very divisive to have a ballot when you are talking about job losses and pit closures, and some areas are terrifyingly badly affected while other areas get off quite lightly. My own gut instinct is to say: yes, once you have a tradition of always holding ballots, you simply have to go along with that tradition. But it is understandable that, given the very strong regional bases in the NUM, you just can't always pull the ballot out of the hat at that stage. It would be a tragedy if, each time MacGregor tackled a particular area, only that area was firm, while everyone else was not prepared to fight. He could carry through his whole job that way without facing a challenge.

If anything, my criticism would be not that the miners haven't had a ballot now, but that there's been too much eagerness to rush into ballots over the last three years, before the issues have built up and resolved themselves in people's minds. It's very easy for the press to move in and put on the pressure. In principle, I'm in favour of ballots, but I am loath to criticize the NUM executive. Their choice is an almost impossible one, particularly when you have the sort of tradition represented by Spencer in Nottingham. The Nottingham miners are not part of the broad sweep of the mineworkers' history. Basically the Nottingham coalfield and the union were created after the General Strike defeat in 1926, and were always seen very much as a bosses' poodle in the inter-war years. The union was only integrated into the NUM at the end of the war, and clearly the traditions of Nottinghamshire live on in the present membership. So there is always going to be a problem in Nottingham, even if you get the rest of the mineworkers solid.

I think one of the most impressive features of this strike, regardless of its outcome, has been the determination of the NUM leadership. The very fact that they have succeeded in shifting opinion is a tribute to the remarkable mobilization of the miners themselves and the fact that a working-class strike of this magnitude polarizes national politics within weeks. It can't be ignored. Another feature, a reflection undoubtedly of the impact of feminism, has been the incredible campaign launched by miner's wives and other women. It is no more a passive tea-making role, but a strong presence on the picket-lines.

The Attack on Local Government

Let us now move on to the question of local government. I'm sure you've already answered this hundreds of times, and yet there will be readers of this interview in other parts of the world who just want to have an explanation of a very simple question: why is this government deciding to attack local government and making it into a central political issue in contemporary Britain?

If you look for a one-sentence answer, there's a slogan I have occasionally seen painted on walls, I think by anarchists at the time of elections: IF VOTING CHANGED ANYTHING, THEY'D MAKE IT ILLEGAL. That's probably a large part of the reason why the Tories have decided to act. For years, whether you had a Labour or a Tory government, at national or municipal level, it was the Social Democrats who got in. But now we've actually demonstrated in London, under the nose of the government and the national media, that voting Labour can produce a different administration. For all our setbacks and failures, no one will allege that we're the same as all the others.

Whereas the government started off with the assumption that a radical socialist administration would be so deeply unpopular that it would be easy to block and defeat and smash it, either by using the judges or even by eventually defeating us in an election, they've now reached the conclusion that we have actually become quite popular. As people have seen the fares policy, the Greater London Enterprise Board and the job creation policies, as they've seen our stance in favour of nuclear disarmament and our campaigns on sexism and racism, there has been not only a change in subjective moods but also a quite consistent movement to Labour in the polls conducted during the three years of our administration. Given the press hysteria, we started with a fairly low base; but now we have got to the point where a GLC election tomorrow would give us our biggest-ever majority. We've currently got a majority of 48 to 44, and if there were a GLC election tomorrow it would be 58 to 34. We would even narrowly win Mrs Thatcher's own constituency in Finchley. That would be such a blow to the present government, such a good example for a future Labour government, and such an encouraging boost for socialism at every level in British life, that I just don't think the Tories want to run the risk of having it written into the history books. The government's own reasons for not having another election do not stand up. First, it argues that it needs to control the local authorities, because we are undermining government economic policies. I wish it were true. If we had that power, we wouldn't hesitate to use it. Were all the twenty hit-list authorities to be abolished and their spending brought in line with government targets, there would still only be a saving of £800m a year – which is peanuts in terms of the national economy, one-half of one per cent of total public spending.

In fact, even if you had a substantial bloc of Labour authorities working together, they would not be in a position where their spending power could dramatically, or even marginally, affect central government policies. If the government wants to get rid of us, it isn't because we are undermining central government policies. We don't have that power, and we would be naive to create the illusion among workers that we can actually protect them.

The second reason given for the abolition of the GLC and the other authorities is that it will cut bureaucracy and save money. But here the Tories have decisively lost the argument: all polls show that most Londoners expect their rates to go up, services to worsen and bureaucracy to increase, and they are most probably right. For if the GLC is broken up and its functions transferred to a dozen different quangos, there will be a multiplication of bureaucracy and most probably a worsening of services. Any saving made through cuts in services will itself probably be offset by the additional bureaucracy, and London will be reduced to a Kafkaesque nightmare. It will be like the 1974 re-organization of the Health Service, when everybody in the country suddenly saw a mushrooming in bureaucracy and a reduction in the actual level of service.

Anyway, we've had Patrick Jenkin[3] wandering around the country, saying to anyone who will listen that this is all to do with the structure of government and stopping wasteful expenditure, and not convincing anybody at all. It was left to Norman Tebbit to be quite honest and blunt about it. He completely undermined all this old nonsense a fortnight ago,

---

3. Patrick Jenkin: secretary of state for the environment in the Thatcher government.

when he said something to the effect that the GLC was in the hands of evil Marxists, practising class warfare on a scale that Karl Marx could only dream about, and that it therefore had to be abolished. Norman does go over the top a bit, and we all love him dearly for it, but although it's a gross overstatement, that is how they see it. They see us as a danger.

In one sense it's true. Thatcher's biggest success has been to persuade a substantial body of opinion in Britain that what she is doing is inevitable: that we've got to have unemployment and hospital shutdowns, that we're living beyond our means, and so on. But in Sheffield, London, Merseyside and the other municipal authorities where things are at least better than in the past, people can see a dozen or so Labour councils posing fairly radical municipal-socialist policies. And when they start looking for an alternative to government policies, they will actually be able to see one in their Town Hall. In many ways what South Yorkshire has done with transport and job-creation, as well as the various things achieved in West Midlands, Merseyside and the GLC are more dangerous to the government than abstract political campaigning.

People in Britain are very empirical in the way they approach things. They aren't going to take a volume of theory off a bookshop shelf and say, I'll buy this tomorrow and we'll transform the world. They move very cautiously. After a period of moderate left government, they will start to become more demanding in terms of socialist policies. I remember that, during all the upheavals in Berkeley in the 1960s, some people who claimed to be revolutionaries would say: 'We're going to vote for Ronald Reagan as governor of California, because if he gets in it will be so awful as to provoke a revolution.' Things don't work like that. If there's a complete collapse of society as in 1917, and you've got somebody like Reagan, the Social Democrats start looking very reasonable. People then go for Social Democracy, and it's only when that starts to reveal its contradictions and failures that you start to see a growth of demands for socialist policies. People are cautious; they don't wish to see the little they have got, lost or smashed in some way. Labour councils demonstrate that you can do certain things without bankrupting people, all the time preserving democratic rights and attempting to involve people in the administration of services. That adds up to a very powerful alternative; and if the government wants to get rid of the metropolitan counties and the GLC, and is desperately trying to control the budgets of other councils, this is not because it would release billions of pounds for arms expenditure or whatever. It is because the action of these councils points towards a very powerful alternative force in society, including at the level of national government.

In other words we are facing fairly ruthless capitalist politicians who are seeking to limit democracy.

If you look at the track record of this government, it has been absolutely ruthless. It knows exactly what it's doing and where it is going. But although it has a coherent strategy, not everyone on its own side of the barrier agrees with it. A lot of Tory wets, for example, are getting very worried that there will be a reaction at some point, and quite a few peers in the House of Lords share that view. They are all in favour of screwing the peasants, but they don't want to screw them so hard that they then turn round and cut their heads off. It is simply a disagreement within the ruling class about how far and how fast it can go. Thatcher has had it all her own way for some time, because the resistance doesn't seem to have been there. But I think that has now changed.

The GLC Experience

When you look back on your entire period as leader of the GLC since 1981, what do you think was the most critical stage for yourself in terms of keeping control of the GLC? It was very tenuous, and the leadership result within the GLC was very close. John Carvel of The Guardian, in his book Citizen Ken, argues that in 1981, after the collapse of the Fares Fair policy, you were actually saved by the bell of the judiciary, whose open assault on democracy made it impossible for you to be removed as leader of the GLC.

In terms of accuracy, John Carvel's book is excellent and I don't think it will be bettered. He has actually been here, and he has done the work of a good journalist. But he's not a politician and he has trouble in understanding how socialist politicians think. So he tends to say that there are various views you could have had, you choose your own.

In politics nothing is ever wholly a defeat or a victory. Even when you think you are coasting home to a great victory, things are probably happening as a by-product of your success which are laying the seeds for future problems and which might mushroom into future defeats. Thus the creation of the welfare state was not simply a victory for Labour: it had benefits for capital as well, which was relieved of the pressure of providing services for its own employees. And now, although Thatcher has had a string of victories, one of their by-products has been a reconstruction of the British Left, a rethinking of how we operate, a realization that in government you have to be more determined. Her attacks have forced socialists to think what they really want out of the structure of local government in Britain. If you are responsible for the day-to-day administration of something, every policy will produce consequences you cannot foresee at the time. We've had many problems arising here on that basis, and our ability to cope with them depends on how open and flexible our learning processes and democratic processes within the Labour Group – on whether we go open-mindedly looking for the problems, or whether we pretend they are not there and reject them. At key points things we thought of as defeats have had important consequences.

The vicious press attacks of the first six months turned us into something that couldn't be ignored. If the press and the government had completely ignored the GLC from day one, it wouldn't have had a quarter of the impact it did have because of their onslaught. There are some parts of the country where the local Labour Party struggles away and the local press has a total boycott of coverage – that is the most damaging thing of all. Although the first six months at the GLC were appalling for those of us who went through them, and although they shook the nerves of the Labour Group, we did learn an enormous amount and become part of the political debate nationally.

As to the judges, they never fail to respond. We've just seen that with their decision on the Association of London Authorities – a case we should obviously have won.[4] And I strongly suspect that if we get to the Court of Appeal, Donaldson will not only uphold the decision of the lower court but actually widen the terms of the judgement to prevent all of our political campaigning. Indeed, Patrick Jenkin has already made a speech calling on the judges to make those sort of attacks if we get into the Court of Appeal. The problem for the judges is that they are so out of touch, simply because they lead a sheltered life and are isolated from all the currents of opinion around them. The London men's clubs, you know, are not the best gauge of public opinion.

The judges moved against us just at the time when opinion was starting to shift in our favour, and because they hadn't

4. The Association of London Authorities was formed in 1983 to represent the interests of local government in London—a task which, in its view, the official London Boroughs Association was not adequately discharging. The courts subsequently ruled that it was unlawful for the GLC and local councils to fund a body whose aims and objectives were drafted in such a way that no Tory authority could subscribe to them.

picked up this slight change in the political climate, they attacked us on our single most popular issue. It is absolutely certain that if it hadn't been for the public reaction on fares, and if a massive campaign hadn't put the judges in the spotlight, I and another thirty would have lost the Camden surcharge case that followed hard on its heels. I'd now be bankrupted and barred from public office for five years. It's like a war: sometimes a defeat will lay the seeds for a future victory. The key to being a successful politician is to skillfully exploit those totally unpredictable issues as they arise. There is always a wealth of advice about the key issues of principle. The problem comes when you have to take a decision within twenty-four hours about something whose full complexity is not at all clear. Then you have to rely on your principles and apply them to a difficult tactical decision.

I agree with you. There was a strong feeling among sections of the left at that stage that all the left councillors should resign. I disagreed with that view. But there is a real problem here, and resignations surely cannot be excluded on principle.

That was understandable. Everyone had come in assuming that things would be a lot easier than they turned out to be, and in the first nine months all the compromises bore on the left of the Labour Group. Much of what we had hoped to do had been chopped, and we were then at the absolute low point. There would have been something wrong if the left hadn't started to ask: should you really stay? Isn't it better to reveal the whole sham? That was largely a view that existed outside. Very few people on the GLC ever shared it, but they realized that they would have to carry the movement with them if they weren't going to resign. They could also see that despite all the defeats, a number of other things were lifting off: the anti-nuclear zone, the peace year, the anti-racist year, and so on. Those haven't had much in the way of coverage yet, but the equal opportunities policy, for instance, is the first real example of its kind, and its general framework could be applied to virtually any other employment in Britain. The Greater London Enterprise Board also had a very slow start, mainly because of officer obstruction. But I never had any doubt that the one key thing by June 1981, when publicity had turned us into a national institution, was that we had to succeed. If we had given up after six months and said: 'You can't do it', and gone into some sort of opposition or resigned, it would have damaged the whole of the Left for decades. There would have been a perception that, well, the Left completely screwed up in six months the biggest thing it ever got its hands on. However bad it was, we had to stay in there, we had to hold on to office (although we never assumed that it automatically meant power), we had to do as much as we possibly could. We have demonstrated that over a period of time you can get a lot of the policies through: you can eventually become popular; you can gradually get control of the bureaucracy (which has invaluable lessons on how to tackle the Civil Service for a future Labour government). If we had quit then we would not be in the position we are in now, where we can point to poll after poll giving us majority support. And not only that. Whereas in general elections London used to be a perfect mirror-image of the national political balance, within two or three per cent of the overall pattern, we now have a ten per cent Labour lead in London, as opposed to nothing nationally. I would never have believed you could get that in three years.

There were moments of doubt when it was really grim, when the hysteria was being whipped up over Ireland or Gay Rights. I remember meeting you in late August 1981, and you were bubbling over with enthusiasm for all the controversial stances we had taken. It was absolutely wonderful to bump into you, because I was surrounded by people saying: 'For God's sake play this down.' The only others who gave me encouragement at the time were some of the people then working on the *New Statesman*. I had a general chat with them once and they said: 'You're absolutely right to have taken up all these things.' A lot of people were prepared to say at that point: 'Well, we should tone these down, and drop them off.' But even on our grants policy, we had a solid base of support of about one-third of the population of London.

I wonder how Professor Eric Hobsbawm and *Marxism Today* would explain our success in winning popular support. They have been advising the Labour Party to move to the right, to win back the departed souls of the SDP, to move towards a coalition with everyone to the left of Edward Heath, and similar sorts of rubbish. Hobsbawm has attacked Tony Benn and myself in public, and even more vehemently in private. I look forward to reading their analysis of why Labour is ahead of the Tories in London and nowhere else in the South.

The Role of the Judiciary

At the height of the political campaign unleashed against the GLC by the judges, we had a very clear glimpse of how the judiciary operates when there is no mass movement knocking at its door. This applies equally to the conservative wing of the judiciary and to its liberal wing. For instance, we heard that senile octogenarian Denning saying: 'Many electors did not vote for the manifesto, they voted for the party. When a party is returned to power, it should consider what is best to do and what is practical and fair.' Scarman went even further and said that the 25 per cent fares reduction had been adopted not because a higher fares level was impractical, but as a measure of social and transport policy. 'It was not a reluctant yielding to economic necessity,' he said, 'but a policy of preference. In doing so, the GLC abandoned business principles. That was a breach of the duty owed to the ratepayers and wrong in law.' In other words what both these old men are saying is 'do not challenge the logic of capital.'

That's right. You meet that broad basic theme from one judge after another. What is interesting—and I knew nothing about the judiciary before I became GLC leader—is that in all our campaigning you come across a judicial angle. We've always had to have one eye open to make sure we don't leave a flank open to judicial attack, and we've also detected how the confidence of the judiciary ebbs and flows. Clearly the judges reacted to the press campaign after Heseltine introduced his bill to control council budgets in 1981, so that by the end of the year they felt they could step in and crush the GLC. Normally, of course, when judges make a political decision, it affects only a tiny percentage of the population: one factory, one trade union or a small minority within that trade union; only seldom does it attack millions of people in such a direct way. In fact, I can't think of another instance where the judges have issued such a publicly controversial ruling that has taken money out of people's pockets.

People suddenly decided that they didn't like it: there was a wave of anger all over London, as hundreds of thousands of people demonstrated, attended public meetings, got on buses dressed up as judges, and so on. Our legal advisers kept reporting that the judges were unhappy about this; they didn't like people mimicking the judiciary, didn't like to be thought of as political. Then Kensington decided to take us to court for not increasing the rents, and although the circumstances were almost identical to the fares issue, we won the case. After a similar victory over the Camden surcharge, there was a whole period of about eighteen months when we won all our court cases. We prepared much better for them and worked into our defences all the ritual things that you have to do to give the judges a way out that will allow them to avoid being drawn into a controversy. But we could already sense that the public reaction to the Fares Fair decision meant that they weren't going to become involved any more.

Now that Thatcher has been re-elected and the government is again introducing legislation to control us, the judges are inching forward again. They've done it on the Association of London Authorities; and they'll probably do it on any other matter on which we come to court. They think that since we're going to lose, they can put the boot in at the end, to teach us a lesson before we go. It really is remarkable that although they are not very sensitive to rapid changes in opinion, judges do broadly follow the political tide. This has been much clearer in the area of trade union legislation—but even then there was the first judgement in the NGA case, which hardly anyone believed to be definitive. You can never be a hundred per cent certain when you go into court. It has been a very valuable lesson. I wasn't aware of just how political the judiciary was.

The Campaign against Abolition of the GLC

What about the present campaign to save the GLC? I was talking to Mike Ward before I came in and he was generating a confidence which wasn't just put on for my benefit. He said that he thought there was a real possibility that the GLC could be saved and that the abolition wouldn't go through because it involved cancelling the electoral principle.

There is a chance of defeating abolition. There is no chance, short of total transport stoppage, of preventing London Transport from being taken away from us. Since there are no constitutional implications and it doesn't affect anywhere outside London, it will sail through the Commons and the Lords. Still, if the transport unions had sufficient support within the garages and the tubes to pull the whole system out indefinitely, it could be possible to force the government to back down—particularly if the British Rail suburban services could be brought out as well. The impact on movement in London would be traumatic and this government's primary concern is the smooth functioning of the City of London. If there is one group of public sector workers who can defeat Thatcher, it has to be the transport workers in London. But my own contacts, from the top of the union tree down to the grassroots, don't suggest that the confidence is there, particularly given what is happening with the miners. They don't really feel like sailing into a political battle with the government.

Equally, I don't think there is a chance of stopping rate-capping. Rate-capping will be amended in the Lords, the general powers will most probably be rejected and there may be some small safeguards built in. But the majority of the SDP and the Liberals agree with the Tories that these twenty hit-list 'wicked Marxist councils' have to be brought to heel. The power that matters, the selective one, will go through, and so the whole movement will be in a major upheaval in the spring of 1985 over whether Labour councils should stay inside the law or defy it. On the abolition, however, things are getting very interesting, because I can't think of any issue where the government has had so little public support for a key element in its programme. All the polls show that no more than 22 per cent of Londoners support them and that over 60 per cent are opposed. This has boosted the Tory rebellion in the Commons and although the government has never been in danger of losing its majority, a number of key Tory moderates like Heath and Gilmour did vote against Thatcher. Heath was actually in quite good form. They will argue that the government hasn't won its case—which is true.

The government's main problem is that we all come up for re-election in May 1985, a year before they can abolish the GLC. Since they obviously don't want to leave us in office for an additional year or two without an election, they have to come up with this idea of abolishing the election and introducing a committee of borough councillors to run it, with an in-built Tory majority. The constitutional implications of that are extremely serious: in the past, whenever a council has been abolished, its term of office has been extended until a successor body takes over. The government's manoeuvre is so blatant and obvious that a lot of moderate conservatives and cross-bench peers are likely to vote against it. But it is pointless trying to count heads in the House of Lords, because they die before you finish the headcount and new ones appear. Currently you've got about 1,250, and the most you can ever get to vote is about 360. What we do know is that the government chief whip in the House of Lords has advised the Cabinet that he can't guarantee to get the abolition of the election bill through. The results of our headcount suggest that it will be fairly close.

Now, if the election goes ahead next May, it will take place at the height of the rate-capping debate, at the height of any industrial action associated with it, and just as the Abolition of the GLC bill is reaching the House of Lords. All the arguments in the House of Lords centre on the point that they can't really overturn a commitment contained in a government's election manifesto. We'll remember that one for the next Labour government. But if the May 1985 GLC elections turn into a referendum over whether to support the retention of the GLC, it will be much more likely that the Lords will be pushed into action to overturn the bill. On balance, there is at best a fifty-fifty chance, but in our electoral and parliamentary system that is a remarkable achievement.

Is there anything that could be done by the PLP and the Shadow Cabinet to slow down the Tories?

They are no better off than the Tories are on the GLC. Unless we are stopped by forces outside this building, we get our way on what we want to do inside it. We can be delayed for a couple of weeks, and we only have a majority of four. But if

we get the votes, we eventually win unless the courts declare
our action to be illegal. It's even more true over there, where
illegality doesn't come into it. If Neil Kinnock got into the
habit of picking up the mace and smashing it on the speaker's
head every day, they would just change the rules to bypass
that. There might be some delay, and the potential for delay
in the House of Lords is much stronger, because there are no
rules there at all. It seems to operate on the basis that things
will go along as they have done for the last eight hundred
years. You could actually put an amendment to the Abolition
of Elections bill to the effect that the interim authority must
guarantee to continue funding organizations x or y. We are
funding about three thousand at the moment, so if we can
find enough peers, we could have them all stand up and make
a speech proposing continued funding of the Gay Teenage
Group and so on down the list. But although that would delay
things for quite a while, it wouldn't get us to the election. The
government has to be defeated. It is true that there's a
chance. I started out thinking we had perhaps a twenty or
thirty per cent chance six months ago. Now I think there is a
fifty-fifty chance in the Lords.

The Liverpool Rebellion

*How would you assess the situation in Liverpool? It is obviously
very different from London, except for the fact that, much to my
surprise, the Left on Liverpool Council does seem to be getting a lot
of public support. The demonstration a few weeks ago was a fairly
large one.*

Liverpool is in a completely different situation from that of
the GLC, in the sense that Labour only won it last year and
inherited a budget cut to pieces by previous Tory and Liberal
administrations. They're now trying to build up from
scratch, just as we did in 1981, but in a year in which the
grant penalties are very much worse. Whereas we, in line
with our manifesto, just increased the rates to the amount
required to fund the programme, the Liverpool party has a

clear policy of not doing that. There is a fundamental tactical difference about the role of rate increases. I don't know what the nature of the rate is in Liverpool. In London one-third of our income comes from the City and Westminster, so it's a wonderful mechanism for redistributing wealth. Sixty-two per cent of our total rate income is from industry and commerce. I don't think Liverpool is in that fortunate position, and I'm not certain what the London Labour Party policy would have been if it had had to evolve in the conditions they face there.

Everything should be done now to support them; we ourselves have made an offer to buy large chunks of Liverpool city centre, to provide them with the funding necessary to get through. If I had a criticism of them, it would be that they haven't adopted the kind of open decision-making process operated in Sheffield and the GLC and many London boroughs. It has been very difficulty to find out the financial facts about their budget, whereas any fool can pick up our documents and work out the GLC budget. It's a big game of monopoly. You *can* reduce difficult financial decisions to a simple intelligible form, which can then be debated throughout the movement. In Liverpool they didn't do that, and you therefore don't know whether Jack Straw was right to say that they could get by with a sixty per cent rate increase, or whether, as they themselves argue, they would need two or three hundred per cent. I don't like to be in that position and there is a risk that if the information doesn't go out to everybody else in the movement, you will eventually alienate support. As things stand at the moment, they have a lot of support. Liverpool is a solidly working-class city with a very organized Labour movement, in a way that London isn't. They haven't got the suburbs stuck in as we have, so it's a much more disciplined city to call on for support. We've had criticism of our broad campaigns from comrades supporting *Militant*, who say that we shouldn't be looking for these wider alliances. That's all very well, but there are probably hundreds of gay refugees living in London away from the sexual intolerance in Liverpool. We have to develop our style of campaigning so that it reflects the composition of the city we represent. Their style wouldn't go down well here, where you have a strong feminist movement and a whole range of community groups, middle-class issue groups and so on.

We'll do all we can to support Liverpool. My only argument has been to say to them: whatever happens this year, get through the year and be in the firing line with twenty others next year, because no other council can actually engineer itself into a Liverpool-type situation this year. We've been able to freeze rents and fares, expand spending by £120m and cut rates this year. There is no way we could get into the Liverpool camp if we tried, and this year almost every Labour council is in the same position. So they are on their own. If I had been in the Liverpool Labour Group, I would have been arguing for them to have the minimum necessary rate increase to get them through this year, so that they will be there with the other dozen or more who will be done on rate-capping next year.

And thus avoid the Clay Cross syndrome, where a council does good things but is then isolated and smashed.

But there are real problems arising from different regional developments. The London Labour Party has consistently argued that rate increases are the lesser of two evils, a tactical necessity, and what has happened on the GLC has proved that case to be right. We are now in a position where we are able to step in and, with a small London-wide rate increase, help prevent Hackney from being forced into a sixty per cent rate increase. Now, after three years, we have learned how to work the financial mechanism of the GLC; and if we weren't facing abolition and rate-capping, my guess is that by this time next year we would be funding a large proportion of borough council spending, thus completely negating the government's penalty system. That is another reason why the government has to get rid of us. We have developed on the basis that we do believe in the rate increase necessary to fund our programme, while a completely different political position has grown up in the Labour Party in Liverpool. There isn't really a way of easily equating the two: they will be equated for us when rate-capping comes in.

Pay Differentials

Still on the GLC, one of the criticisms that has been made by all sorts of people is that the employment of lots of lefties, very good people by and large, on these whacking great salaries, doesn't do the image of the GLC much good. I have heard that David Blunkett in Sheffield succeeded in cutting them down a bit, but that has not been attempted here. Isn't it a bit ludicrous that X or Y is getting a giant salary compared even with skilled workers?

The lowest-paid white-collar worker in the GLC is on about £5,000 a year, and the highest-paid, the Director General, is on £40,000 a year. Looked at in those terms, it is not a massive differential. In the private sector the equivalent salary for one of our controllers would be £60,000 to £70,000. This year we did the same as last year: we offered a weighted wage increase, giving ten per cent to the low paid and one and a half per cent to top officials, but with a cut-off at £31,000, so that no one over £31,000 would get an increase. They went to abitration and have just been awarded a 4.9 per cent increase. We are built into a system of trade-union wage negotiation which means you cannot just come into office and say: we are abrogating top salaries. There is no easy point at which you can come in and say 'these are the baddies, and they are getting too much', because the people on the tier immediately underneath them are expecting to get that much with their next wage increase, and the knock-on effect goes all the way down. For each of our three years we have narrowed the differentials by giving a wage increase above the rate of inflation for the low-paid, and below the rate of inflation for top salaries. Over a period of five or six years such a policy would largely erode your problem.

The real difficulty is not that we pay the Director General £40,000 a year, but that when we create a post like that of the Head of the Ethnic Minorities Unit, we pay the successful candidate £22,000. But we have a career structure here which has been built up over years of negotiation; and if you create a post in the bureaucracy which is at a lower level than its equivalents elsewhere, it doesn't carry the status. A major struggle through the first two or three years was to ensure that the units we created had clout here within the bureaucracy, and it was difficult enough to do that without saying that their grades should be lower than those of the people in the bureaucracy with whom they were negotiating, and most of the time fighting. We were also under constant pressure from the unions and the staff association, which complained that we weren't paying enough for the posts that we were creating. Nobody has got a socialist wages policy. But I must say I think there is an awful lot of hyprocrisy about this: somebody once wrote a great letter in *Labour Weekly* condemning us for our outrageously high salaries, and a couple of months afterwards we went along to see the individual concerned, saying that we were setting up a particular unit and would like him to come and work for us, and he demanded £20,000 a year. I have my doubts about the sincerity of some of the critics. You can only really complain when you have been offered it and turned it down. A lot of people we are employing donate part of their salary to political organizations they are connected with. You can't specify this an an employer, but many of them do, because they find the salaries embarrassing.

What sort of remuneration do the councillors receive – you yourself, for instance?

Full-timers, including myself, get £6,000 a year: about £4,000 from the daily attendance allowances, and £2,000 from special responsibility allowances.

So in fact the elected representatives of London get a small salary . . .

Less than a sixth of what the officers are paid. So I would be all in favour of narrowing differentials.

It seems that there has been a great deal of upward mobility for left-wingers who have taken non-elected posts at the GLC.

You get the problem that when we advertise these posts, half the time the left doesn't apply. We have denuded a lot of Britain of its resident left-wing population, because they have all come to work for us. But there is still a great lack of left-wing managers: we are all polemicists and ideologists and meeting-packers; we're not much good at managing bureaucracies. People like Reg Race have been a godsend, because for the first time the flow of information to councillors is as we would wish it to be. You couldn't bring Reg Race in and say: well, we're bringing Reg Race in but we are going to halve the salary, because immediately you would dramatically undercut that person's status. It would be ideal to have a building where the status didn't rest on what your post was or the money you were paid, but it does. It would take a decade or more to change the ethos of the bureaucracy of the GLC. If we hadn't been involved from day one in a great struggle with the government, we might have had more time for trying to change more of the bureaucratic structures and mentalities here. But we have been under such pressure from outside that we haven't had the time to sit down and start the fundamental re-examination of the way this bureaucracy works. Besides, a lot of the trade unions involved are rather antagonistic to many of the changes we have made. The opposition to our policies on racism and sexism came from our white-collar staff association, and they bitterly resisted for two years. That always seemed to us a more important issue than the question of salaries.

Employment and Housing Policy

You have been criticized from some quarters on the grounds that GLC policies seem somewhat tailored to the pressure of the public sector, while other sectors of the working class are served less well by them.

I don't think you can say that we as an employer shouldn't improve the quality of life for our employees, particularly when that involves weighting wage increases in favour of the low-paid. If we could find a way of insisting on a minimum wage London-wide, we would do that. But the fact that we don't have the power to affect low wages outside this building doesn't mean that we can't do something about it inside. The fact that we can't ensure pre-school childcare for everybody's kids outside doesn't mean that we shouldn't press on with doing that inside. The examples you set do allow trade unions outside to make the same demands for themselves. The government has fed the general theme that people in the public sector are basically lazy and molly-coddled, and some groups on the left have made the mistake of taking up the same theme. I don't think this has happened often: it has generally remained a gutter-press complaint. But there is a bias.

It should be realized that over the last twenty years, the pattern of employment in local government in London has shifted dramatically. Whereas twenty years ago the average borough employed an equal number of white- and blue-collar workers, in many boroughs that has now shifted to 60 per cent white-collar against 40 per cent blue-collar. A series of policy issues taken up by officers has done a lot to change the pattern of employment. We discovered here, for example, that the question of herbaceous borders has been a key class issue. In London's parks, herbaceous borders have been systematically removed by London Parks' administrations. All over London you find flowerbeds grassed over, shrubberies pulled up, so that all you have to have is someone sitting on a bloody great lawnmower, zipping all the way round it. End of park duty. Vast numbers of gardeners' jobs have been lost. Councillors have very seldom been consulted about this: it has just been a question of normal day-to-day parks' management. A lot of antagonism has therefore built up, as white-collar jobs have burgeoned and blue-collar workers have lost theirs. One of the growth items in our budget for this year is that we should start to restore herbaceous borders in our parks, because it is labour-intensive work, and you get a much better laid-out park. This is just one example that we stumbled on in a report: when I asked why the herbaceous borders were being removed and we all kept worrying them for an answer, we were eventually told that it was to save money by getting rid of blue-collar jobs.

The same thing has happened in one area of the public sector after another. The white-collar bureaucracy has protected itself very well and has not really done anything to protect its brothers and sisters in blue-collar jobs. Some of the antagonism that has built up was obvious during one of the major debates in Lambeth about what should be done to resist the government's pressures. All the women employed in the social service manual grades, the home helps, were brought together to discuss the question at a meeting addressed by Ted Knight. Their basic call was: if you want to get over this crisis, sack some of the penpushers. We can deride that as the wrong reaction, but they had been watching the penpushers doing O & M studies and getting rid of their jobs for year after year, and the movement had never done anything about it.

We need to say now that all the policies on estate management over the last thirty years have been wrong. There should be a little office on each estate, with someone sitting in a proper entrance to a block of flats in the way that every private block of flats has. These are massively labour-intensive areas. There has never been any debate on the left about the pattern of local employment. We've fallen into voting for increases in spending which lead to an increase in white-collar jobs and do nothing for blue-collar jobs. Look, too, at the squalor on our streets. When I was a kid the streets were swept every day, but I cannot recall from the thirteen years I have been on local authorities any debate about the level of street-sweeping. It's been left to officers to manage, and so we've seen a massive erosion of jobs that really matter to working-class people. I can understand how the idea builds up that some sections of the public sector have been molly-coddled.

Could tenants on GLC estates be encouraged to provide facilities for themselves to repair and maintain their houses? Is there not a lot more scope for that?

I think there is. I don't believe there is a way in which Hackney and Lambeth can manage their property in a socialist manner, given that they are each trying to manage some fifty or sixty thousand homes. It is beyond the capability of individuals to manage an empire like that. The Freshwater Group couldn't manage their property and it wasn't just that they were property speculators. You just can't manage that scale of organization. You have to break it up into manageable units. If a unit is sufficiently manageable, then people can manage it themselves. They will employ their own local maintenance team. That would involve a major upheaval for the building unions involved. It would quite possibly cut against their immediate interests, but in the long term it would create thousands of new jobs.

I would just like to raise another aspect of this whole attack by the government on the GLC and the metropolitan counties. Some people have argued that a subsidiary reason for abolition is that without the GLC and the metropolitan counties, it would be far easier to isolate and smash the public sector unions.

There is clearly an element of that. But if I was the government and my objective was to break the public sector trade unions, I wouldn't have wasted a year trying to abolish the metropolitan counties. I would have gone for compulsory privatization. In its wildest fantasies the government cannot envisage getting rid of more than ten thousand jobs through abolition. But if it really went to town by compelling councils to put things like housing management out to tender—which is what Wandsworth is experimenting with at the moment— hundreds of thousands of jobs could go. They could get rid of more jobs simply by squeezing education authorities on school meals provision. There are much easier ways of getting rid of jobs than local government reorganization.

What sort of reaction have you had to the plan for the Royal Docks? Why has the GLC adopted this approach?

We have always proceeded on the basis that even if we don't have those particular powers now, we may eventually get them, and therefore you have to do that work. The Enterprise Board, the Industry and Employment Committee within this building and its Popular Planning Unit have been looking, sector by sector, at the whole question of employment in London, so that if a Labour government is elected in a couple of years' time, we will have done a vast amount of the groundwork and research for an immediate employment-creation programme in London. The Royal Docks is a part of that. We have drawn up a plan that is completely opposed to the present London Docklands Development Corporation, which is little more than a speculator's plan to get the maximum speculative development out of the area. We've drawn up a pattern of development which would be mixed and beneficial to the whole community. It may all look very academic now, if we are going to be abolished. But Newham is still there and will plug away at it, and a Labour government will be in a position overnight to sack everyone on the Docklands Development Corporation and to appoint nominees to implement our plans while the repeal of the GLC abolition bill is going through. You never know when success is going to come. Three years ago to this day, the Tory administration signed a deal for a huge speculative office development at Coin Street, on the basis that work had to start within three years. I never would have believed at the time, as we were fighting it through the committee, alleging corruption and all else, that three years later joint council and community action would have prevented anything happening at all. We're now in a position where they have opted out and sold the land back to us, so that we can start drawing up new plans for the site. I can't see any immediate chance of winning on the docks. But three years ago I saw no chance of winning on Coin Street, and we became the owners of it yesterday.

The Tasks of a Left Government

Could we now return from local government to the Labour Party? Benn said at a recent fringe meeting of trade unionists that 'Of course our task remains one day to refound Labour as a socialist party.' What do you think he's getting at?

I see what he's getting at. There are all these currents running through the Labour Party which have gone through a very bad nine months wondering what the role is for the Left. And now they are slowly starting to coalesce around the objective of making sure that we get control of capital in a future

Labour government, that we get control of the Cabinet, that we set the objective that the candidates were selected for. These are the short-term tasks, but there is also a growing understanding that the whole nature of the Labour Party needs to change, in terms of bringing trade unionists back into it in a big way, shifting to workplace branches that can draw organized labour back into the movement, making sure that women's or black groups can affiliate directly, and so on. We are in a period when, although not much is going to change in constitutional terms, a major backlog of demands is building up. I think we will have a major shift in the structure of the Party, which will have the effect of basically refounding the Labour Party. It will be the first real reconstruction of it since 1918. The structure has become quite outmoded and there is a growing demand for change which could build up into a very powerful force over the next two or three years. I do think there is a real chance that in 1987 or '88 a quite dramatically radical Labour government will come into office.

The next thing I wanted to ask flows from that. What would you expect from the next Labour government? What should be the first three or four measures it should push through? That is, in a period of six to eight months.

Six to eight months? You need a lifetime, given the bureaucracy. I think the key will be the style that we set. Whatever Labour government is elected, it is going to suffer defeats, because of the power of capital, and the obstruction of the civil service, the media and the judges. The key to the whole success of the government will be the imposition of its will on the City of London. If it fails to do that, it will inevitably fail in the long term. It will be too late after the election. We have to go through the election campaign saying: 'We will pay for the reconstruction of our economy by controlling capital.' The question is whether that will be done through nationalization of the banks—which is unlikely given the balance of forces within the leadership—or through very strict controls and the direction of investment. It is much more likely to be the latter than the former. In one sense, nationalization of the banks would not change anything, unless the Labour government took detailed control of the direction of investment and ensured that huge amounts of money were not simply funnelled into some large National Enterprise Board. The government will have to set targets for the money going into each sector of the economy and involve the workforce in the planning of its allocation. Information technology, in particular, will be the crucial area of the economy at the turn of the century, but there is still life in the medium term for British manufacturing and for an expansion of the iron, steel and coal industries. A major programme of reconstructing the welfare state will create a real demand for the sort of basic industrial products which have been most dramatically cut back. In the short term, the only way to tackle the problem of unemployment is to direct investment into the creation of a lot of new jobs in the industries which have suffered the major contraction, whilst preparing the investment for the new jobs that will dominate Britain in the 1990s. But if the Labour government does not approach the City of London with confidence and impose its will, the City will detect any weakness and surge forward. Then there will be the usual run on the pound and the breaking of the will of the party.

The key thing is to make sure that the funding of our programme is quite clear from the start. There will have to be an attempt to check the flow of capital out of the country, which will begin as soon as Labour gets ahead in the pre-election polls. But that won't be decisive: for although every rat will take everything they can get their hands on and run out of the country before the polls are closed, the constant process of generation of new capital goes on, and the state of our economy is so bloody weak anyhow that it is questionable how much of it can be used in the first year. In retrospect our failings at the GLC have been due not so much to financial constraints as to our inability to spend the money and gear up our programme. In our first budget, which we brought in after our first year in office, we massively underspent. We had the money, but we hadn't got the workers in place and the programmes drafted to carry it all out. I should imagine that the same problems would affect a Labour government: however much work has been done on the programme, it won't have been done in the detail necessary to transform it into a programme of economic action. That is the key to everything.

The second crucial task will be to make it clear to the judiciary that things have changed, although I'm not clear in my own mind what the exact package of reforms of the judiciary should be. The judges won't be a problem for the first six months to a year, because they will have recognized that the government is there and that they can't do too much. But when the government starts to get vulnerable, slipping in the polls or losing a couple of by-elections, the judges will start giving their difficult judgements and then there will be a lot of braying from the Tories about obeying the law that could cause a Labour government some major embarrassment. So, I would want to see a programme for the reform of the judiciary there on day one. Among the things it might include would be early retirement, at the age of 65; the selection of judges from solicitors rather than just barristers; or perhaps a system like that of some European countries, whereby you don't just go from public school to Oxbridge to the bar and then on to the bench, but you actually have a profession of being a judge. People should leave school and train to be a judge, and in that way a much wider social range of people could be brought in. The key to it would be to sack Donaldson in the first few days. He is such a total Tory. I don't know how old he is. If there were a retiring age of 65, a lot of vacancies would immediately be created and it would be possible to start changing the political complexion of the bench.

The third vital task is to deal with the press. Nobody will be elected in Britain for advocating state control of the press, but I think that an emphasis on access and balance could be acceptable. We should say to the public: why don't we have the same controls on the press as we have on ITN? Although we all see the bias in ITN in terms of its establishment approach, the reality is that it would adapt to a new establishment approach over ten years of Labour government. It is broadly establishment, and broadly social-democratic rather than Thatcherite.

Alistair Burnett is not a Social Democrat . . .

No. But in terms of the broad ethos of radio and television, it is social democratic. Our immediate problem is the popular press. The radio and television report what the press has laid down as News, and an extension to the press of the balance requirement in the Independent Broadcasting Acts would immediately remove from the *Mail* and the *Sunday Express* all the blatant party-political distortion. At the same time it should no longer be possible for anyone to buy up a newspaper, and each of them should be turned into co-operatives run by the workforce. Certainly no one in Britain is going to fight in the trenches to defend Rupert Murdoch's right to run the British media. However, if those co-operatives are to be viable, it will be necessary to ensure that people placing advertising should not be allowed to discriminate on a political basis. What sunk the *Daily Herald* and the *News Chronicle* wasn't that people weren't reading them, but that people weren't advertising in them. Advertisers boycotted the Labour press. There would have to be a law that no one launching a new Sierra or running a Guinness campaign could bypass a paper they didn't particularly like. Anyway, once political balance has been secured in all of the media, the advertisers won't have anywhere else to go. That would change the whole climate, the whole day-to-day ethos. It would mean that the people at ITN or IRN would not be looking at papers filled with the usual crap: there would be a gradual improvement and perhaps some real journalistic standards would begin to develop.

Finally, there is the key question of access to radio and television. The board of governors of the ITV and the BBC will have to be changed so that they are more reflective of the community as a whole, and measures will have to be taken to greatly extend access to broadcasting and to introduce much more in the way of regional and local programmes. Complete access should also be allowed to a range of new radio stations. In London, for example, it would only cost the GLC about £250,000 to initiate and get running twenty or thirty radio stations. I don't want to see the present Tory media replaced by something reflecting the views of Len Murray or Merlyn Rees or whoever would be put in charge. There isn't a right or a wrong political answer on anything. We need diversity, so that people can pick and choose.

It is interesting, particularly in light of what later happened in Russia, that Lenin once devised a scheme for a state printing corporation whereby if any group of citizens above a certain number—about 50,000 signatures, I think he specified—came to this corporation and said that it wanted to produce a newspaper, regardless of what it was, the state should have a duty to produce the paper for them. That is very radical. In Sweden they have state subsidies for all political parties to produce their own newspaper: the larger the party, the greater the subsidy. Trotskyist, Maoist and libertarian groups all get a very large subsidy from the Social Democratic government to produce a newspaper and some publications. That is something worth considering.

All these things can be done. If the Labour government is to survive, it will have to impose its will on the City, it will have to take out the judges who are opposed to it and it will have to take out that constant poisonous drip drip drip of propaganda from Fleet Street. Then there will be time to get one's policies across, without being beleaguered from day one. Changes must also be made in the Civil Service. Thatcher has brought into the Civil Service a number of appointees who share her political perspective; Labour has to replace them. We then have to say that the Civil Service must be opened up. Anybody should be able to apply for any job in the Civil Service. There must not be a situation where people come into it from school and university and are moulded by it. It needs to be made much more dynamic. You would have to break a lot of the racism and sexism in there, and that will involve a degree of confrontation with the trade unions concerned. You will also have to bring in not just key people at the top, but key support teams of advisers for each minister—from the trade unions, the academic world, the parties, etc.—and start to find the radical elements within the Civil Service who have undoubtedly been keeping their head down waiting for better times.

A careful study should be made of how the ministries operate. It is not enough just to put in a new minister: you've also got to find at least ten people to assist that minister, running the bureaucracy. But even with a proper support team, it will take two or three years before they start to get control of that bureaucracy. One thing that would help would be to say that we, as socialists, want to see Parliament as paramount. Power has shifted from the floor of the House of Commons, where it really was in the last century, to the Civil Service. Whereas present governments can set up a bill committee and pack it with hacks, it must be possible for any government producing a housing bill, for example, to have it scrutinized by MPs who know what they are talking about. There should be a whole series of committees which hold the

Civil Service accountable *and* check the Labour government and make it a proper legislature. At the moment it's a bloody circus. These are all points about structure, rather than about policies, and of course I would not like people to think that I am not interested in policies but the structures need to be changed for the policies to survive.

There is one thing related to this and that is the way in which the nationalized industries work. Surely we need to institutionalize some form of self-management in these industries, so that the workers have the right to elect the people who run them. If the Civil Service wants to propose MacGregor against a candidate from the NUM, then let them do it. Both will put forward their case to the workforce and we'll see who is elected. I'm sure the media would go hysterical at such a change, but that, in itself, would be educative.

If we don't do something to popularize control of the nationalized industries, it will never be possible to persuade any other industry that it should be nationalized. We keep losing this argument about nationalizing banks at the Labour Party conference because at the moment the bankworkers don't want to be nationalized. They have their cheap mortgages, they're doing very nicely and they are looked after by their employer who keeps them sweet for fear of that. They have seen what has happened to the steel and mining industries, and they don't want to be nationalized. What happens is that the state comes in and smashes you into little bits. Everyone shouts about Clause Four or public control of the media, but we all forget the phrase about 'under popular systems of administration'. Public ownership is often unpopular, both in the nationalized industries and among the tenants on the receiving end of Tower Hamlets Housing Department. There is not a popular system of administration.

A Left Foreign Policy

*Before we finish, we must discuss some questions of foreign policy.
The CLPs have voted now for many years for a neutral, non-
aligned Britain, for withdrawal from NATO and for a policy of
giving some leadership to the Non-aligned Movement. This is a
critical question for the Labour leadership, and the union bloc vote
has always been used to vote that out. There is no doubt that
de-nuclearization and the removal of American bases would be a
big leap forward in itself. I think, however, that the question of
how much money is spent on conventional armies and weapons—
which can cover such things as nerve gases—should not be over-
looked. The official leadership of the Labour Party is very weak
on these issues, and it has been argued in particular about the
current leaders of the party that, despite the fact that they have
said they wouldn't press the nuclear button themselves, they would
give the go-ahead to the incumbent in the White House to do so.*

I think that is unfair. When I compare Kinnock with his
predecessors, the things which give me greatest hope are his
statements like: 'I won't press the button.' If he had said that
to the Labour Party conference, you could dismiss it as
empty rhetoric. But when he says it to a private closed
meeting of American Congressmen, that makes more of an
impact. That is Kinnock saying: 'I don't agree with you on
the direction in which you are taking the world.' I also
remember seeing Kinnock interviewed by David Frost. At
one point, Frost said: 'so you see things as most people do,
that the major threat to world peace is Russia.' And Kinnock
replied: 'No.' He said that both sides were equally to blame. I
think he may have said, America more so than Russia. No
previous Labour leader would ever have said either of those
two things. Kinnock has grown up in his times, which have
been largely anti-American in Britain. He has been involved
in a whole series of campaigns against American foreign
policy, and it might be easier to win him to a more progressive

foreign policy than to a more progressive economic policy.

But could I remind you that it was written into the Labour Party Manifesto for the 1964 election that they would get rid of Polaris. Wilson always argued against Polaris and made a whole number of attacks on American foreign policy in South-East Asia. In 1967 I compiled a tiny little book for Private Eye *called* The Thoughts of Chairman Harold, *in which I went through everything he had said from the late fifties to 1964. It was quite strong stuff. Wilson talked in 1954 of being on the side of the Vietnamese revolution against the Americans.*

Dominating the whole of the Labour Party leadership from the time of the Cold War has been a total pro-Americanism. That has now changed because the most fanatical pro-Americans defected to the SDP, and I think that you are likely to see Kinnock genuinely move into neutralism as quickly as he can go. That may sound very Gaullist. I think I can detect among the British Left a growing tide of neo-Gaullism, and it has a mirror image on the other side of the class divide. I do a lot of speaking to institutions, which are one of the influential areas we have targeted to try and persuade them that the GLC shouldn't be abolished. In the question-and-answer sessions you stray on to all the other things like Ireland and Gay Rights. I have found that there is a growing feeling in the City of London that alliances are not permanent. The mere fact that we've been in one with America for forty years doesn't change that. A growing body of opinion within British capital sees that its own economic interests probably lie in a common European approach to developing the Russian economy and to breaking away from the American one. The client relation we have to the Americans is now damaging their economic interests. If a Labour leadership started to move into a generally more neutralist position, looking for an opening to Russia, it would get a response not just from neo-Gaullist elements on the British Left—which has always reflected a lot of anti-American chauvinism rather than anti-imperialism—but also from elements inside British capital.

Isn't this the new European position, held by the German Social Democrats and other Eurosocialists? They represent anti-Americanism, but from the standpoint of European capital.

Over the last few years, America has become increasingly hysterical about the economic links between Western Europe and Eastern Europe and the Soviet Union. This goes right back to when Willy Brandt became Foreign Minister in the Bonn government in 1966, when you had this grand coalition and an opening to the east. It has been a recurrent theme in Germany and France, where politicians could be quite offensive to the Americans and go east looking for an opening. There is a real prospect that towards the end of this century Europe will re-orientate itself towards Russia, with America turning much more firmly towards Japan and China. Or perhaps we will see the emergence of Japanese–Chinese and other great trading blocs, with the real risk of world war for trade reasons. That is a danger that we haven't really faced since the Second World War because of the American dominance of the world economy.

What allies would you see for a Labour government that is going in a socialist and anti-imperialist direction?

As I already mentioned during our last conversation, I've never been violently anti-EEC, because I've always had a streak of that *Socialist Organiser* philosophy that such a stand always slips into nationalism. If tomorrow there were the prospect of a united Europe, with a pan-European Parliament and Socialist Party, I would take it immediately. My objection to the Common Market is that it is so very unpopular that it makes any genuine concept of European unity infinitely more remote. So I would not write off strong links with European socialist parties. I think this is something we should try to achieve.

But who do you relate to? Would it be the Socialist Parties, the Communist Parties, the Greens or the Peace Movement?

In a sense, you know, the British Labour Party encompasses both Eurocommunism and the Greens. Hobsbawm may still formally be a member of the CPGB, but his influence is strongest within the Right of the Labour Party. It is hardly accidental that he is approvingly quoted by leader-writers on *The Guardian* and *The Observer*, two papers sympathetic to the SDP. There is also a strong Green current within the Labour Party. The Socialist Environment and Resources Association pre-dates the formation of the British Ecology Party, which is well to the right of even the right-wing of the German Greens. Our own orientation in the GLC, and that of Blunkett in South Yorkshire, is very strongly 'green'. Peter Tatchell has recently written a very powerful socialist defence of an ecological orientation. The point I'm making is that the broad left (in the best sense of the word) in Britain is, essentially, inside the Labour Party. In Western Europe it is split up into separate parties. But enough of Europe. I'm not an expert and I've resisted all pressures to stand for the European Parliament, which is a fake body. What I look forward to is a Labour government committed to help transform living conditions in the Third World.

A socialist foreign policy would surely involve more than developmental orientations. It would mean providing material aid (including weaponry) to the Central Americans, openly defending Nicaragua against the might of the USA, providing facilities for the liberation movement in South Africa, returning Diego Garcia to the Mauritians, and so on. I don't see how that can be done without a fundamental change. Britain may not have many colonies, but it is economically an imperialist country. Labour should, at the very least, fight for a Swedish or Austrian model on the foreign policy front, but one should not underestimate the difficulties.

Fine, but that still leaves out the question of alternative trading blocs.

That poses the fundamental question of the social system. Why should British capital help to develop Nicaragua, except in a limited fashion and for narrow reasons of self-interest?

You'd have to develop and strengthen existing trading links, but based on the principle of equal exchange. There is a large number of Third World countries with which we would not be very satisfied ideologically, but with which there is no reason for not trading in a new way. A major drive to develop the Third World economies would, I think, be a direction in which we should go. But clearly we could do that far better if it were part of an all-European initiative, than if it were just a question of Britain on its own.

It is also necessary to scale down Britain's defence spending. One of the dangers with all this stuff about nuclear weapons is that people start saying we need a larger conventional force. We don't. What is an effective deterrent to invasion is to have a popularly based army which would fight a guerilla war if we were invaded. If a potential invader knew that five million people in Britain were trained to fight a guerilla war street by street, it would certainly think twice. Look at the impact of the North Vietnamese on America, or the Afghan tribesmen on Russia. A long, drawn-out guerrilla war is a tremendous strain on the economy of any power. Not that there is any reason why Russia should invade Britain. Either you invade the whole of Europe, or you don't invade any of it. What I do think we should do is back the liberation movements quite firmly. I would relish the prospect of a Labour government getting elected and immediately sending massive aid to Nicaragua and forcing the Americans to live with that or break off relations.

There seems to be a major conflict within the Party on the question of 'black sections', that is, the right of black people in this country as an oppressed minority to organize their own units within Labour in order to combat more effectively the institutionalized racism that undoubtedly exists inside the organization. The attitude of many Labour politicians towards black people has varied between racism of a fairly explicit sort and a more old-fashioned paternalism. This latter is still pretty rampant, especially in the midlands, where the Labour right tends to treat Asian ghettos as their private rotten boroughs. The GLC has pioneered a novel propaganda campaign against racism, which has undoubtedly had some impact. How do you perceive the debate on black sections?

I think that the main opposition to black sections comes from those labour MPs who have, over the years, voted for racist immigration laws in Parliament. Their argument (and that of the Tories) was that if you let less black people into Britain racism would automatically decrease. Accordingly Britain has passed more immigration laws than any other European country. The result has been the exact opposite of what was argued. Racial discrimination has increased tenfold.

A subsidiary fear of the Labour Party establishment is that black sections would immediately come under the control of the *Militant* (*chuckles*). This is especially ironic given that *Militant* is strongly opposed to the idea in the first place.

Both views are wrong. It's simply no good a white-dominated party in a white-dominated society telling black people how to organize themselves. I think that racism is so deeply ingrained in British society that every white person (regardless of subjective intentions) has a degree of racial prejudice. Labour politicians who genuinely want to combat racism should start listening to black people.

In order to work out the best method of fighting racism black people need to be able to meet, discuss and organize collectively. Of course they will not agree with each other on many issues, but they could work out a common plan and corresponding structures to challenge racial inequality. The presence of whites, however well-intentioned, would inevitably alter the nature of the discussion. Our limited successes in the GLC have been because in each case black officers, black groups and black people have told us what needed to be done. We simply responded. This is an important start and any mistakes committed are by their very nature educative for all concerned.

From this you can gather that I don't believe anyone has anything to fear from black sections in the Labour Party except those who, for whatever reasons, are reluctant to challenge the institutionalized racism which is so deeply embedded on every level that it has become almost 'invisible'.

Should we end there?

Yes, I'm exhausted. But it's been extremely useful.

Appendix One

Tony and Ken, the natural leaders that Labour needs but can't have

Richard Gott

There are only two figures in the Labour movement who are natural leaders, men who can encapsulate in words and images the often inarticulate aspirations and hopes of hundreds of thousands of ordinary people. They talk the language of common sense. They fill halls and command audiences on television. And they do so because they tell things the way they are, and the way they ought to be. Needless to say, in our perverse political system, Tony Benn and Ken Livingstone are not at present candidates for the vacant leadership of the Labour Party.

Instead there is a Gadarene rush by ambitious placemen to fill the yawning gap. Before anyone has had time to draw breath, or even to read the rulebook, we are presented with an unappetising choice — between a Yorkshire gasbag and a Welsh windbag—and told that, lump it or leave it, this is to be the destiny of the Labour Party. No Latin American colonel, organizing his *coup d'etat* on the telephone, could have acted so swiftly. No People's Republic central committee, camouflaging dissent within its ranks, could have behaved with such aplomb.

A timetable is rolled out as though written on tablets of stone: nominations in by mid-July, a final choice in October, and then, heigh ho—a thousand cruise missiles later—a General Eelection in 1988 in which, it is confidently assumed, the Labour Party will recapture the so-called middle ground. All those nice video-and-Volvo SDP supporters, and all those flag-waving Tory skilled workers, will come waltzing back into the Labour fold, attracted by the effortless prose of the Pied Piper of Hattersley or the florid strains of the Mull of Kinnock.

This is the old-style Labour Party in full fig: the party of Ramsey MacDonald and Lord George Brown, the party of the block vote and the fudged manifesto, the party of the tower block and the destroyed inner city, the party of the macho joke in the workingman's club, the party of ideas in opposition that fails to put them into practice in government, the party of the Bomb, of the Vietnam War. It is a party that has taken a long time to die. Its putrefying corpse still poisons the present and casts its baleful shadow over the future.

Many of the most unsavoury elements have already gone off to join the SDP, a kick-down-the-ladder-now-we've-climbed-up party designed to preserve the privileges of the well-heeled middle class, a party of authoritarian wolves in de-centralist clothing, a party that may have begun in the centre but seems destined to end up well to the right of its current Liberal ally.

But many of this ilk still remain, conservatives in the mould of Denis Healey, John Silkin and Peter Shore. They had their chance to run the country in the Wilson and Callaghan years from 1966 to 1979, the years that the locust devoured. They had their moment in the sun, their chance to put their mark on history. And their failure was dismal to behold. Exhausted and without credibility, they virtually forced the votes into the Thatcher camp for lack of an alternative.

Opportunities of the kind they were given then do not come round a second time, and, belatedly, most of that dreadful gang have agreed to slink soundlessly from the scene before a worse fate befalls them. But they have left a legacy behind them, they have sown the dragon's teeth. And suddenly springing from the fertilized soil come new champions, Roy the Harold Wilson look-alike, Kinnock the Michael Foot clone, history's tragedy repeating itself as farce.

Must this go on forever? Must Europe's standard-bearers against the infinite wiliness of the Right always be drawn from a class of opportunist pragmatists, men who have begun to treat with the enemy even before they've got a foot in the stirrup? Must the sad story of François Mitterrand, of Felipe Gonzàlez, of Mario Soares, of Andreas Papandreou be repeated over here?

Is there never to be a chance for those with a vision of real change to be given the opportunity to lead the troops into battle? Is it forever unimaginable that the Left could provide itself with a coherent revolutionary programme at least as radical and convincing as that with which Mrs Thatcher has armed the Right? And find itself a leader to match?

For beneath the country's calm, even complacent exterior, revolutionary times are brewing. Mrs Thatcher is about to take the nation on a roller-coaster of a kind it has never been on before.

To oppose her vision of the future we desperately need a party that looks capable of peering into the 21st century, a party that no longer pretends that we live in the imperial era with the map painted red, a party that can rubbish the nuclear deterrent theory as once Martin Luther rubbished the Pope, a party that can envisage detaching us from the evil coils of the superpower Cold War, and a party that can unite around policies and a programme commensurate with the task ahead.

The SDP, which might have played such a role, has marched resolutely in the opposite direction, and under David Owen it will quicken its pace. The Liberals still emit gasps of sanity and under a new Lloyd George (Celtic blather plus political genius) could probably produce reserves of historical strength with which to mobilise the nation. But the Labour Party remains the only party capable of analysing the spirit of protest into constructive and revolutionary change – if it is well led. And for the moment there doesn't seem much chance of that.

This article was published in *The Guardian* 17 June 1984.

Appendix Two

Frontlines

Tariq Ali

The Guardian has traditionally been a liberal newspaper. Its correspondence columns remain the freest and liveliest in Fleet Street, despite the odd lapse. This posture is made easier by the fact that competition is virtually non-existent, unless one considers the *International Herald Tribune*, a minority taste confined to London. A significant section of *The Guardian's* readership consists of what one can only refer to as a captive audience: liberals, radicals, socialists, peaceniks, feminists have nowhere else to go. They can be taken for granted. The result is a mixture of laziness and complacency, which often makes the paper insipid. The pungency is rarely directed at the consensual establishment in British politics and culture. The targets are usually the left inside the Labour Party, the trades unions and, last week, the activists of the Liberal Party.

The scourge of Farringdon Street is, of course, Peter Jenkins. His slipshod arrogance is based more on his established monopoly of newsprint rather than the intellectual strength of his arguments. His politics are those of the average civil servant: a staunch believer in the present economic system; an even more ardent supporter of NATO, nuclear weapons and most other preferences of the Establishment. He is *The Groaniad's* most self-conscious columnist, which imparts to his writing a certain pomposity, mercilessly parodied behind his back by less reverent junior colleagues. He is the pride of bourgeois rationality, the voice of reason and moderation. In short, the thinking person's answer to Bernard Levin.

Last week his column was more demagogic than usual and bordered on vulgar abuse. His chosen quarry was not the dreaded Bennites in the Labour Party. This time he was on the warpath against troublemakers in the Liberal Party. You know, those crazy people who refuse to believe in the infallibility of Fleet Street's favoured politicians. In the old days Jenkins used to froth regularly at the outrages of the 'polycracy'. This was a reference to the hordes of polytechnic lecturers who had supposedly taken over the Labour Party and displaced the political giants revered by Jenkins. This ugly elitism was allowed full reign by *The Guardian*, whose hierarchs agreed with his views.

Now it is the turn of the Liberals. Peter Jenkins, we should mention, is a partisan of Dr Owen and the SDP gang. His message to the Liberals is that they must curb all radical instincts. Since they might be on the threshold of power, the time has come to clean the stables. David Steel's batman Richard Holmes tells Jenkins that the Association of Liberal Councillors reminds him of the Militant Tendency. Jenkins can see what he means. What does he mean? Why not explain to the *Guardian* readership and prove the point? Why bother, though, when half-baked innuendos will suffice?

There then follows a reference to the 'lunatic fringe' and Liberal activists are denounced as 'single-issue zealots, freaks, wuthering idiots' etc. This is supposed to be rational argument. The reference to lunatics is particularly interesting. Its genealogy takes one back to feudalism, where any serf who dared express dissent was declared mad and either chained for life or simply killed. A modern equivalent is the Stalinist bureaucracy in the Soviet Union, which also finds its 'lunatic fringe' unacceptable and consigns dissidents to psychiatric hospitals. Of course, no such remedies are being proposed here. The aim is merely to stigmatize those with whom one does not agree.

Jenkins is not alone. Two days after his column, *The Guardian* published the ravings of Terry Coleman on the Liberal Party Conference. These were headlined as follows: 'Who Selected These Creatures, And In What Sense Are They Liberals?' Clearly not in the same sense as Mr Coleman, who interviews Tory Cabinet Ministers in a tone akin to sycophancy, but treats the Liberal Party activists with contempt. Like Jenkins, he too is pleased that the Leader can ignore all unpleasant decisions. Coleman rants at the decision to demand a troop withdrawal from Ireland, but is probably ignorant of the fact that Irish Unity/Home Rule is a Liberal Party position that goes back to Gladstone. He is particularly shocked at the presence of the Nicaraguans. What right, he thunders, have they here? The article is neither funny nor well-informed. It is merely an apologia for David Steel.

What do these people want? Politics without parties or parties without a thinking, critical membership. Why not, in that case, do away with political parties altogether? MPs could be elected at seasonal gatherings by media pundits and City financiers, and the choice of Prime Minister could be the result of a special election conducted at the US Embassy in Grosvenor Square. If the problem is finding members who are docile and only there to adorn the TV screens during standing ovations, then it would ease unemployment if extras could be hired through Equity (the actors' union) when it is time for the annual conferences. We could dispense permanently with Peter Jenkins's lunatics and Terry Coleman's creatures and get down to real politics. Surely that is what democracy is really about, isn't it?

This article appeared in *Time Out* 29 September – 5 October 1983.

Appendix Three

Monetarism in London

Ken Livingstone

In May 1979 when Mrs Thatcher came to power, there were 132,000 people unemployed in Greater London.* In September 1982 there were 390,107. This amounts to a trebling of those without a job. For London as a whole, when allowance is made for unregistered women and for commuters, approximately one-eighth of London's workforce is now unemployed. In Inner London, the figure is one in six; in Stepney it is one in three. These figures amount to nothing less than an economic scandal.

This collapse of employment has taken place against the background of a world economic recession which struck all industrial countries severely in the mid-1970s and re-emerged in late 1979. But what figures from the OECD clearly show is that the British slump has been much more severe than those of the non-monetarist industrial countries. Faced with slow economic growth, Mrs Thatcher's response has been to engineer the deepest economic crisis that Britain has known since the 1930s. She succeeded in actually cutting national wealth by 7% by the end of 1982, and, at the very moment when this wealth was declining, consciously favoured the financier against the industrialist, the employer

*This report was submitted, on behalf of the Labour Group, to the Greater London Council on 12 October 1982 and is reprinted from the Council Agenda. An appendix on redundancies has been deleted.

against labour, and the rich against the poor. In just over three years since she came to power unemployment has increased by over two million, from 5.4% to 14.6%. If we add in the estimates for the unemployed who are not registered (mainly women), total unemployment is now over four million people. In this project her charts have been made out by a coherent economic theory, prepared over 25 years and multinational in its scope and organization. Its first trial run at a national level was in Chile from 1973 under the guidance of General Pinochet. Not until 1979 did monetarism – for that was the theory in question – sit at the cabinet table of an advanced industrial country.

In Britain, the monetarists had made London their main bridgehead. In the mid-1960s Milton Friedman's Chicago school took over the master's economic course at the London School of Economics, whose graduates were to staff many of the country's university and polytechnic economics departments. London's financial journalists followed a few years later, together with an increasing number of city financial advisers. It was the crisis of 1974 and 1975, and the clear uncertainties of orthodox Keynesian economic policies which gave monetarism its major political opportunity. The propositions of the monetarists are simply stated: (1) That inflation is a purely monetary phenomenon and can be cured by restricting the supply of money in the economy. In practice this means raising interest rates (which reduces the demand for money) and cutting state spending to try to lower the Public Sector Borrowing Requirement (PSBR). (2) That poor economic performance is the result of imperfections in the markets for 'real' products, and can be cured by removing monopolies and restrictions. The three main restrictions were held to be the unions, the state and international protectionism. Hence the attempts to weaken union power, cut and privatize state activity and remove exchange controls, the protections of a low exchange rate, and preferences for national purchasing by state bodies.

What this amounted to was an attempt to restore the value of money at the expense of wage labour. This was made explicit in the approach of the London Business School, one of whose leading monetarists became Mrs Thatcher's chief economic adviser. If inflation was a major problem then the answer was to cut state spending and the social wage. If unemployment was the issue then the way to solve it was to cut the money wage. The proposed mechanism was the following. First interest rates were to be raised. This would attract in international money which would force up the exchange rate. A high exchange rate would make exporting more difficult and attract imports. This would put pressure on firms, further squeeze their profits and make it impossible for them to agree to increases in money wages. In the corporate world, the weaker would be expected to go under, leaving the fittest to survive. The increase in unemployment would put further pressure on labour to accept lower wages and abandon improvements in working conditions which had been gained over the previous decades. Cheaper labour and higher productivity would help restore the profit rate and economic activity.

Engineering the crisis

This was the essence of Mrs Thatcher's monetarism for the private sector. It was spelled out before the election, and on many occasions since. It has also been followed in practice. The 11% interest rate which held at the time of Geoffrey Howe's first budget rose to 17% within a year. The exchange rate which had been at less than 1.60 dollars to the pound in late 1976, and at 2.07 at the time of the election, had risen to around 2.40 dollars to the pound by late 1980. The severe reduction in internal demand together with the adverse exchange rates squeezed all the producers of traded goods, particularly in manufacturing. Industrial output fell by 12%

between 1979 and 1981. Manufacturing profits from a 1978 level of 6.8% fell to 2.1% in 1981. Unemployment rose from 1.3 million at the time of the election to 2.5 million in mid-1981 and now 3.3 million in September 1982.

Those who have gained from this conspicuously-engineered crisis have been the banks and the oil companies. Finance capital is now in the ascendancy in spite of the protests of industrial capital both privately and through the Confederation of British industry. Crucially, monetarism has weakened labour in the private sector. With redundancies and unemployment rising, workers have had to settle for declining real wages and worsening conditions at work. Many unions found their membership falling as unemployment rose. Some of the larger industrialists indeed stuck with monetarism in spite of the squeeze because of its successful weakening of labour.

In the public sector, the manipulation of markets is a blunter instrument. High interest rates raise the cost of public services, but for the most part cannot bankrupt them. Nor can the international market be summoned to discipline the state as it has done private industry. Selling off state enterprise, even government research establishments, has been one response – but is possible only with the profitable entities and they are not at issue. Privatization of services (like refuse collection) is another, whose principal success has been a decisive reduction in the security of employment. But in spite of these attempts to introduce the rule of the market into areas which had been developed by the state because of the failure of the market, the bulk of state production remains insulated from such forces. Instead, direct spending ministers, notably Mr Heseltine, have tried a succession of direct disciplines, cash limits, penalties, even threatened prosecutions. Their aims were cuts in the social wage, and in the power of labour within the state sector. But partly because of the resistance of local authorities to these measures, and partly because of the action of public-sector workers organized nationally, monetarism has been much less successful in the public as against the private sector. This was Mr Reagan's main criticism of British monetarism when he met Mrs Thatcher shortly after he became President. It was a weakness that Chile did not exhibit (they cut state employment by 30% between 1973 and 1976, and nearly halved spending on health, education and housing by mid-1975), and which Mr Reagan, too, was determined to avoid.

Finally, there was the question of the money supply itself. To Mrs Thatcher's chagrin, in the first two years of her government it kept on growing. This was in part because of state spending. In spite of the cuts, in real services, the Government's policies resulted in major increases in debt charges, unemployment and social security payments, and spending on defence. This drove up the PSBR to unprecedented levels. In addition, the squeeze of the private sector forced companies to expand their borrowing. They were buying time by mortgaging their assets, even though the new money, taken as a whole, reflected asset values which might never be realized in the market place. Inflation actually rose for a time: only after the destruction of firms and the demand for credit has inflation finally dropped. Its current level does not reflect the effectiveness of controlling the money supply directly. The Government has notably failed to do that. Rather it is by forcing the economy into a major recession that the Government has caused a collapse in the demand for money and therefore the incentive for its supply.

The Deindustrialization of London

For London labour and industry, monetarism has created the worst economic conditions for nearly a century. Though London was hit by the recession later than other parts of the country, since early 1980 unemployment has risen faster in London than in the country as a whole. While unemployment in the country as a whole has risen by 157% London's unemployment has gone up by nearly 200%. London's manufacturing industry has been decimated as factory after factory has been closed either by the receiver or by some corporate head office. The list of London redundancies of over 50 workers notified to the Manpower Services Commission (MSC) reads like a roll call of the dead. The last major industrial employers have all but disappeared from Tower Hamlets and Southwark, from Islington and Camden, from inner south-west London and from Lambeth. At this moment, the Council is trying to prevent the closure of the last major firm in Hackney and the last plant in Brent. What is striking from the map of the redundancies is how major losses are being suffered by the outer industrial boroughs, Kingston and Hounslow, Ealing and Enfield, as well as the inner city.

Most of the losses are in private sector firms, and, from the evidence we have, it was the induced slump which was the major cause of closures. The MSC conducted a survey of 21 redundancies of over 100 employees in 1981 and found that 13 of the firms gave inadequate demand as the reason for job loss. The remainder of the firms appear to have rationalized their production process, their location, or both. In 1980 the London Chamber of Commerce reported on an 'unparalleled increase' in the number of firms reporting decreasing orders, though the fall in demand was notably worse domestically than on the export market, and was particularly bad in the traditional consumer-good industries (motor and transport equipment, other metal goods, and the furniture sector). By July 1981 business expectations had picked up, but 70% of firms saw the lack of demand restricting output (compared with 40% in June 1979). In spite of a reported optimism, succeeding surveys have shown that there has been no sustained expansion of activity. By mid-1982 investment remained static, domestic orders were on average on the increase but the large firms were facing big falls in export orders 'almost verging on a collapse'. Overall, the fall in domestic orders appears to have been most severe in the period October 1979 (when 19% of firms reported decreases in orders) to July 1981, after which there was a slow upturn. Export orders and production levels followed a similar pattern. This it will be noted is the period of high exchange rates.

A further factor behind the closures was rationalization following mergers or takeovers. The MSC surveyed 124 redundancies in the second quarter of 1982 and found such rationalization accounted for 20% of the redundancies, a level consistent with their surveys over the previous 12 months. From the experience of the Council over the last six months, this general picture is confirmed. Of the ten fac-tories facing redundancy who approached us, five faced a slump in domestic demand, one was reorganizing production in the light of a change from electro-mechanical to electronic products, and the remaining four relocated production (two to the South-West, one to Wales and the other to Scotland) as the result of over-capacity rationalization, or, in one case, a move financed by government subsidy to an area of weaker labour.

The list of redudancies also reveals a loss of public sector jobs in central government in public utilities and in local government. Barking (443), Lambeth (798), Bromley (836), Camden (596), Wandsworth (273), Croydon (80), Barnet (68), Lewisham (200), Havering (275), Sutton (54), and Greenwich (50): these redundancies made in response to the cuts in local government expenditure total more than 3,500 jobs, and exclude the loss of jobs accounted for by natural wastage. The loss of employment in local government has not been so severe as in manufacturing: there has been successful resistance to cuts in a number of boroughs by councillors, unions and local campaigns. But those jobs that have gone have tended to mean not merely a loss of work, but a decline of services as well.

Service industries more generally have been weakened by monetarism. Tourism which had grown in London in the 1970s was severely affected by the high exchange rates from 1979. From 8.4 million overseas visitors to London in 1978, the number fell to 7.9 million in 1979, to 7.4 million in 1980 and 6.9 million in 1981, an overall decline of 18% between 1978 and 1981. A similar slump took place in the construction industry as both public and private sectors cut their investment. In all, between 1979 and 1981 of the total redundancies reported to MSC (95,386), two-thirds were in manufacturing, and the remainder from construction and services.

What is clear from this evidence is that the current economic crisis is affecting London in a quite different way to the last great depression of the 1930s. In the 1930s the depression struck at the regions which had gained from the expansionary phases of nineteenth-century industrialization: the textile workers of Lancashire, the coal miners and steel workers of Wales, Scotland and the North and the shipbuilders of Belfast, the Clyde and the North-East. London and the Midlands were saved from the worst effects of the depression by the growth of new manufacturing. Of the increase of 644 factories in Britain between 1932 and 1937, London accounted for 532, and this was the continuation of a trend stretching back to the early 1920s. In mid-1932 London's employment was 18% up on its 1923 level, whereas Wales—the worst hit region – was 31% down.

Yet it is these same factories which are now being closed. Hoover in Perivale and Firestone in Chiswick are two of the most celebrated names of the 1930s to have closed since 1979, but there are many more on the great industrial estates of West and North London. The results, as in the depressed regions in the 1930s, are a cut in jobs (down 8% in London between 1978 and 1982) and growing mass unemployment.

In July 1982 male unemployment in Hackney was 22%, in Poplar 31% and in Stepney 32%. The unemployed of the East End do not have as far to march as the Jarrow workers in the 1930s. But their plight is increasingly similar. The inner cities are the depressed areas of the 1980s.

Women and Monetarism

Women are adversely affected by monetarism in all the ways outlined above and more. In the main, women are the managers of the household economies and in increasing proportions they are heads of households in their own right due to divorce, single parenthood and widowhood. Women have also been an increasingly important factor in bolstering family wages by the huge increase in part-time earnings, particularly among married women. Women are also the primary users of the welfare state and recipients of the social wage. Cuts in services have secondary effects on the ability of women to seek or retain employment.

National wealth is continuing to decrease. The effect of cutting the money supply is high interest rates, and low investment leading to decreased public borrowing and spending cuts in services and unemployment, reduces the Gross National Income which is comprised of wages and social wage. Depressing wage levels leads to poverty and poor work conditions. The social wage is made up of state services, such as health, public transport, education and benefits. The depression of wages that follows restricting the money supply reduces inflation and automatically reduces the value of index linked benefits. Although the overall rate of inflation is currently about 8.5% it has fallen less for people on low incomes. This is due to the rising price of commodities such as housing and public transport which take a disporportionate amount from low paid incomes.

Trends in employment and unemployment affect women and men differently because of their, on the whole, unequal relationship to the labour market. The vast majority of low paid, temporary and part-time workers in London are women. The low paid are six times more likely to be unemployed and remain unemployed. Employers have taken advantage of monetarist policies to contain and control the low paid. The Government supports this trend by abolishing protective legislation.

Destruction or Restructuring?

Mrs Thatcher claims that this forced recession is necessary. For her only the discipline of a slump would distinguish the strong firms from the weak and undermine what for her was the key imperfection in an otherwise self-balancing market system: organized labour. This fits precisely with the traditional functions of an economic slump when faced with a crisis of profitability: (i) the writing down of fictitous capital values built up during a period of expanded credit; (ii) the reorganization of production and the increase of productivity; and (iii) the weakening of the power of labour. These are the factors which have regularly restored the rate of profit and permitted accumulation to proceed. They involve a restructuring of the economy at the expense of labour.

Certainly, monetarism has partially carried out these functions. For the country as a whole real wages are now lower than they were when Mrs Thatcher came to power. In London the real earnings of manual men and women were lower in 1981, than they had been in 1977. Whereas 29,000 days were lost in labour disputes in 1979, by 1980 it was down to 12,000 and last year to 4,000. In London, the London Chamber of Commerce and Industry (LCCI) reported that whereas in June 1979 35% of their sample firms reported that labour shortages were a constraint on output, by July 1981 the figure had fallen to 2% and strike activity to 1%. In mid-1982 one respondent was quoted as saying that there was now 'more labour available and less militant than in the past

10 years'. In the private sector at least, it has proved very difficult to organize against closures or redudancies following bankruptcies. In this sense Mrs Thatcher has been successful in using money as an instrument of control.

She has also had a modest success in writing down capital values through bankruptcy, though productivity increases have been less clear-cut. In one sample, two-fifths of the 331 firms said there had been an increase in labour productivity in the period of 1980-1, but an equal number said there had been a decrease. New investment on average remained static during the last three years, and circumstantial evidence suggests that major new manufacturing investment takes place away from London rather than within it.

But there is a real question – from the viewpoint not of labour but of private capital itself – whether restructuring and the restoration of the profit rate can any more take place through the crisis mechanisms of an earlier phase. We are no longer in the economy of the corner shop. London's economy is now intertwined in international webs of production and exchange. So severe would an international collapse of credit be that there is a real question of whether the socio-political structures of the industrial countries could survive. Even in the 1930s, the depth of that crisis, its implications for unemployment, welfare, totalitarianism and eventually war, convinced the guardians of international finance that they could no longer allow a major banking and corporate collapse. The US Federal Reserve Bank was at last constituted to act as a lender of last resort (a capacity it used to prevent a major collapse in 1974). Other central banks which had not already done so followed suit, and in 1945 Bretton Woods was set up to act as a quasi-international lender of last resort.

As the rate of profit fell in the industrial world through the sixties and seventies (in the UK the fall was sharper and earlier than most from 13% in 1960 to 2% in 1982), and as credit expanded to offset a fall in demand, so the central banks acting as guarantors of the banking system provided the state money that was at the root of inflation. What has frightened these same bankers about monetarism is that first Mrs Thatcher and then President Reagan appear bent on bringing about this credit collapse. It is striking that the Bank of England have consistently acted to modify the effect of Mrs Thatcher's monetarism on the interest rate and the money supply. Like the major clearing banks, it has operated an intensive care unit for threatened firms and organized restructuring directly rather than leaving it to the market. The Bank of International Settlements on the world scale have declared themselves in favour of incomes policy rather than the profound dangers of monetarism, and these same bankers have only with difficulty persuaded President Reagan to extend further credit through the IMF to roll over Third World debts.

Economics of the Looking Glass

What the central bankers have themselves realized is the danger of an economic crisis far greater than occurred in the 1930s, and of economic policies in the US and the UK which are consistently pushing the world economy nearer that brink. In short, for a general restructuring to take place the extent of the crisis would be so large as to endanger the economic system itself. This is a measure of the issue which is at stake with monetarism. Furthermore, in Mrs Thatcher's own terms, monetarism at a national and regional level has been an economic catastrophe. It is now clear that the extent of the damage to the British economy was much larger than anyone in the government originally intended. The increase of interest rates bankrupted some firms and forced others to borrow, thus expanding the money supply (M3). The fall in economic activity reduced tax revenue, increased unemployment payments and worsened the budget deficit but at the same time raised the cost of Government borrowing, so that the Government was borrowing more simply to service its debts. Inflation which had stood at 11.3% at the time of the first budget later reached 20%. Demand – already cut by the recession – fell further as firms reduced stocks (and therefore their intermediate demand) in the face of high interest rates. Government advisers were divided as to what was going on, but the Prime Minister carried on inflexibly regardless of the cost. The final cost in terms of employment has been a loss of 2.35 million jobs between 1979 and mid-1982. Unemployment has risen from 1.3 to 3.34 million in September 1982. While industrial production was falling in Britain from 1979 to mid-1982 by 16.5%, in France and Germany it remained constant, while in Norway it rose by 8% and in Japan by 1.2%. Manufacturing employment fell by nearly one-fifth in the UK, far more than that of any other industrial country.

What this has meant is that the industry destroyed by Mrs Thatcher's monetarism is leaving room on the markets not so much for the firms that remain in this country as for those who have kept up production, technical progress and investment overseas. Imports have increased so that this year Britain had a trade deficit on manufactured goods for the first time, as the *Economist* pointed out, since the beginning of the Industrial Revolution. For London this is particularly serious. The output lost from the factories that are being closed is not being replaced by new factories sites in the city. Where new production is taking place it has tended to be in the smaller cities, along the M4 corridor, or in rural towns. For London the loss of these factories cannot be seen as restructuring but destruction. The point holds for the country as a whole, but even more acutely for its capital.

Nor has the reduction of real wages helped British competitivity. The exchange rate policy meant that British manufacturers lost 50% of their price competitiveness in 1979 and 1980, and have since regained only about one-third of this. While workers received less, their effective cost in relation to labour elsewhere has increased. This is the economics of the looking glass. Nor does Mrs Thatcher – from the viewpoint of those interests she represents – fully recognize the effect on national productivity of the run down of public services, of education, of health and of the transport system. Particularly serious for industry and employment has been the wilful destruction of skills and the network of Industrial Training Boards. In road transport and engineering, for example, where skills are vital to any economic revival in London, the number of apprentices nationally was halved from 2,260 to 1,100 between 1979 and 1981. Already by 1982 London's employers were reporting restrictions in output because of the shortage of suitable skills.

On almost every major issue the monetarists have been wrong in theory and in practice. They regard Britain's wages as a problem when they were among the lowest in Western Europe. They regarded taxes as a problem when they were near the average of our competitors (and when by December 1981 Mrs Thatcher's fiscal policy had according to her own figures nearly doubled the tax paid by the average family man). They saw expanded state spending as a problem when in fact many state services had actually declined in physical terms over the previous decade. They saw state debt as a problem when in fact it was at its lowest real rate for nearly a century, rising only now the monetarists' fixed interest indebtedness has increased the real rates of interest paid now that inflation has fallen. In the end they have only been able to cut the money supply and the PSBR (their two initial targets) by massive economic destruction.

To ordinary Londoners this performance appears an economy without sense. Nearly 400,000 are now registered as unemployed at a cost minimally estimated at £3,500 per head per year, or £1,400,000,000 in total. Factories lie empty, land is unused. Machines – often quite new – are frequently being sold for scrap. Ideas for new products in universities, poly-

technics and both private and public industry remain un-
developed because commerce is bad. The sheer waste of it all
is so evident when compared with the needs that are so
patently unmet. If industrialists and the CBI protest, how
much starker is the reality of this destruction to working, or
would-be working, Londoners.

Restructuring for Labour

The Council is necessarily limited in its response. But in its
industry and employment policy it is pointing the way to an
alternative which if followed nationally and internationally
alone holds promise of avoiding the catastrophe which the
central bankers fear. It acknowledges that restructuring
must take place but that it must be a restructuring organized
on behalf of and with the support of labour rather than at its
expense.

The key to this policy is technology. In most spheres there
is a spectrum of new technologies, some centred on human
skills, others aimed to de-skill. The Council has fostered a
new programme of technology networks to make the resources of London's higher research institutions available to
workers wishing to develop human-centred technologies.
These will raise productivity – indeed the lathes and production systems being developed at the University of Manchester Institute of Science and Technology promise to increase productivity more than methods which remove skill
from the operator. This increased productivity is the basis for
those working this new technology to be paid an adequate
wage even when their product is subject to competition from
low-wage countries. Whether in older plants or in new fields
(such as cable development or energy production) these
choices of technology and of ways of producing a given effect
are quite evident to the people working there.

What has to be done first is to stop the destruction of
existing jobs. We have taken the first step in this direction

with our saving of Austins at Leyton and Third Sector in Willesden. In both cases, we have advanced money to cover the cost of the factory, as well as working capital in the form of a loan. The latter has been based on the Council providing finance up to a grant limit of £20 per job week, on the grounds that an average industrial worker in London produces £160 value each week, stimulates a further £40 worth of London production through a multiplier effect, and furnishes a return to the public exchequer of on average £70 per week. A basic financial support of £20 a week is modest. What is needed is for the Government to agree to provide the equivalent of unemployment and social security benefit for each worker whose job the Council saves.

Secondly, we are seeking ways to put together the resources which have been left idle by monetarism. The new built factory programme has been a start here, but we are looking to ways of using such buildings to house production by the unemployed geared initially at each other and the Council rather than at the market. Here, the iron discipline of profit need not enter since – with wasted resources – the private economy's productivity is zero. In many job creation schemes there is a danger that every job created is also a job lost, that a new scheme financed by a public authority will merely reduce the market (and the employment) of the competitors. Within the economy of unused resources there is no such danger. Each job created is a job gained for there is no competition with the market producers.

Thirdly, we are trying to preserve some of the apprenticeship schemes run by the Industrial Training Boards and to defend the skills of which the workforce of London has been so rich a repository. The preservation and expansion of skills we see, along with many industrialists, as a necessary condition for any economic expansion, however introduced.

Finally, we see the need to develop new sectors and new products, ones geared to the real needs of ordinary

Londoners. Our work on human-centred cable system and on an alternative energy strategy for London are the first major steps in the London industrial strategy, together with detailed work in conjunction with the unions on how the furniture industry and different parts of the engineering industry can be restructured for labour.

What is needed to carry out these policies is a capacity for direct intervention in the process of restructuring companies, production methods and products. The Greater London Enterprise Board is developing this capacity, both in the corporate and technology sphere. Important, too, is the Council's programme for Popular Planning, which is aimed to ensure that ordinary people can discuss their needs as consumers, as residents or workers and can play a part in industrial restructuring. But these policies will only mitigate the effects that monetarism has visited upon London's economy. What is needed is a change of government, and the adoption not of a mere generalized reflation, but of a detailed, interventionist policy of restructuring for labour along the lines that we are developing in the Council.

This article first appeared in *New Left Review*, no. 137, Jan./Feb. 1983.